From The Hidden

You Will
Understand It PERFECTLY

Part 1 - Investigation of the Four Horsemen

Part 2 - Understanding the End of the Age

by Anne T. Garcia

From The Hidden—
You Will Understand It PERFECTLY
Copyright © 2005 by Anne T. Garcia
Revised 2006 - Copyright © 2006 by Anne T. Garcia

ISBN 0-9762087-2-5

Anne T. Garcia
From The Hidden
www.fromthehidden.com
email: contact@fromthehidden.com

Published by Waymaker Publishers
P.O. Box 1481
Fenton, MO 63026
Phone: 866.618.2609
email: (waymaker@sbcglobal.net)

From The Hidden
Copyright © 2004
Xulon Press

Dedication

In Memory of
Two Heroes of the Faith

Pastor Woody Shelton
and
Pastor Ron Cullen

Men of Whom the World
Was Not Worthy.
This book is dedicated,
with great love
and deep affection,
to their widows.

Esther Shelton
and
Phyllis Cullen

In Everything Give Thanks

I gratefully acknowledge the following persons who helped in some way with my book, <u>From the Hidden—You will Understand It PERFECTLY</u>.

Firstly, thanks to my greatest friends now and forever, I love you dearly and appreciate you so much — my husband, children and children-in-law, Mike and Kristi, Tony and Andria, Joey and Jamie. Blessings and gratitude to Carolyn Reinneck and the Monday morning prayer group, and Bonnie Wallace and the Tuesday morning prayer group who coined the phrase, "a copy on every coffee table."

I wish to extend my heartfelt thanks to Pastor Willie Moore, Evelyn Kinsella, Pastor Jack Harris and Dr. Debra Peppers for help along the way. I also thank researcher Alice Akley, copy editor Gwen Reeser, typist/translator Juan Eskadon and prayer partner Dorothy Schwarz for all their help. I wish to give special thanks to Dave and Joyce Meyer who encouraged me when I needed it the most.

My husband joins me in thanking the missionaries and pastors who volunteered to take <u>From The Hidden</u> into the nations. They include Jeremiah and Tara Jacobs, Mark and Joanie Akers, Dan Salas, Steve Smith, and Alex and Bonnie Wallace. May any blessing that proceeds from this book accrue to their account.

Words could never express my gratitude to my publishers, Keith and Donna Cherry. Their expertise in marketing, research, technical advice and input on all things artistic made this book possible. Eschatologically speaking, Donna truly is my alter ego. When we're discussing end times, we can finish each other's sentences.

I wish to enjoin a special word of appreciation to my husband Cas. You have allowed me to go forward, all the while covering me in prayer. When you awaken in the middle of the night to pray for me and our children, I see. More importantly, God sees. You are my intercessor "extraordinaire." I love you. We have always stood in agreement on this: If there be any commendation (or criticism) of this work, any soul saved, any life changed...if we have gained any praise, let it be laid at the foot of the cross of our Lord Jesus Christ.

Anne T. Garcia
Summer 2005

Table of Contents

Prologue

In 95 A.D., banished to the island of Patmos because he would not die, John, the beloved apostle, was given a panoramic view of things to come. Jesus' revelations to John are called, in Greek, "apo" (**from**) "kalypsis" (**the hidden**). Thus we refer to the final book in the Bible as the apocalypse.

God has many mysteries. The *"mystery of the ages, Christ in you, the hope of glory,"* (Colossians 1:27) had been revealed through the apostle Paul a generation earlier. The *"mystery of iniquity"* (2 Thessalonians 2:7) still flourishes in the earth today. The *"mystery of God"* will be completed during the seven year period of the Tribulation, according to Revelation 10:7.

One of the most enduring questions Bible students have desired to understand throughout the ages is this: Who are those four horsemen of the apocalypse? They parade across history in Revelation Chapter 6. Many theories as to their identity have been suggested. We will examine them in this book in light of these words of Jesus not often considered in reference to the horsemen: *"It is also written in your law that the testimony of two men is true."* John 8:17

And so we ask the question: Where, besides in the Book of Revelation, do we find the four horsemen? There must be a second witness. Could it be the secret of their true identity is hidden somewhere in the law or the prophets?

Even after we uncover the identity of the four horsemen, our quest has only begun. Where do we, the glorious Church, fit into the end time equation? Did God really promise to remove the Church from the earth, before the Tribulation begins?

Revelation knowledge flows progressively throughout the Church Age. As the time draws near, we see end time events more clearly. The Tribulation is a time when God's righteous anger is fully unleased.

> ²⁰*The anger of the Lord will not turn back until He has executed and performed the thoughts of His heart.* ***In the latter days you will understand it perfectly.***
>
> Jeremiah 23:20 (emphasis added)

In this scripture Jeremiah gives us a startling promise: we will understand it perfectly. In other words, we who live at the end of the age will have the ability to understand perfectly events that will soon transpire.

God is our Perfect Father. He wants us to understand the Tribulation before it begins, because He wants us to escape. As we will see in this book, it is a time more terrible than any other period in human history. In fact, the Lord actually steps in and shortens the time of Tribulation. He does this to save the human race from extinction (Mark 13:20).

We will not delve into every plague, earthquake and judgment in this book. The purpose of this book is to give the reader an overview of the times we live in.

In some cases, we have presented highly speculative explanations. This would include our interpretation of "666" and the image of the beast. The reader is encouraged to apply the admonition of Acts 17:11 to everything in this book. Namely, to search the scriptures and see if these things are so. Soon the Book of Revelation in your own personal Bible will be well-worn, underlined, starred and annotated. This is good.

The Book of Revelation is the only book in the Bible that begins and ends with the promise of a blessing to those who read it. In Revelation 1:3, John is the one who offers us a blessing, In Revelation 22:7, it is our Lord Himself who promises us we will be blessed if we read Revelation. Dare we ignore the words He Himself has spoken, knowing that the time is at hand?

Part I - An Investigation of the Four Horsemen

CHAPTER

1

FTH

God's Divine Week

The universe is approximately 14 billion years old. This is a fact upon which scientists and the Jewish sages generally agree.[1] Somewhere in those past ages ancient animals roamed, urban populations flourished, and then a cataclysmic event occurred.

This is clearly recorded in this Biblical record, in verse 2.

> [1]*In the beginning God created the heavens and the earth.*
> [2]*The earth was **without form, and void;** and darkness was on the face of the deep. And the Spirit of God was hovering over the face of the waters.*
> [3]*Then God said, "Let there be light," and there was light.*
>
> Genesis 1:1-3 (emphasis added)

Notice in verse 2 that darkness covered everything. God took the prophet Jeremiah backwards in time and showed him this dismal scene. Many scholars believe verse 2 refers to the destruction of a pre-Adamic civilization, which resulted from satan's rebellion against God. Here is the way Jeremiah recorded it:

> [23]*I beheld the earth, and indeed it was **without form, and void;** And the heavens, they had no light.*
> [24]*I beheld the mountains, and indeed they trembled, And all the hills moved back and forth.*
> [25]*I beheld, and indeed there was no man, And all*

> the birds of the heavens had fled.
> ²⁶I beheld, and indeed the fruitful land was a
> wilderness, And all its cities were broken down,
> At the presence of the Lord, By His fierce anger.
> ²⁷For thus says the Lord: "The whole land shall be
> desolate; Yet I will not make a full end.
> ²⁸For this shall the earth mourn, And, the heavens
> above be black, Because I have spoken. I have
> purposed and will not relent, Nor will I turn back
> from it."
> Jeremiah 4:23-28 (emphasis added)

The blackness persisted throughout eons of ages until God's appointed time. And then, when it pleased Him, He gave the command in Genesis 1:3 *"Let there be light"* and the Light of the World came on the scene. Notice Genesis 1:14-18 records the creation of the sun, moon and stars did not occur until the fourth day. The light that came forth on the first day was the Light of the World, the Lord Jesus Christ:

> ¹In the beginning was the Word, and the Word was
> with God, and the Word was God.
> ²He was in the beginning with God.
> ³All things were made through Him, and without
> Him nothing was made that was made.
> ⁴In Him was life, and the life **was the light of men**
> ⁵And **the light shines in the darkness**, and the
> darkness did not comprehend it.
> John 1:1-5 (emphasis added)

And so, six thousand years ago God created Adam and gave him dominion and a mandate to rule. We know the story all too well. Let us summarize human history from Adam to this present day.

From Adam to Abraham 2,000 years – Age of Conscience.
From Abraham to Christ 2,000 years – Age of the Law.
From Christ to the present 2,000 years – Age of Grace.

Human history has one more age to enjoy, namely the Millennial

(1,000 year) Reign of Jesus Christ, before eternity begins.

I like the way Kenneth Copeland puts it: "For all practical purposes, 2,000 years have come and gone since Jesus' birth and ministry. Six thousand years since Adam was created. You and I are being squeezed between 6,000 years of time behind us and another 1,000 years ahead of us. The 1,000 years facing us is the Millennial reign of Jesus of Nazareth." [2]

And this, dear readers, is what is known as "God's Divine Week." But you may consider a week to be a span of time that covers seven days, while I am speaking here of a span of time that covers 7,000 years. A single verse of Scripture can quickly erase all confusion.

> *[8]But, beloved, do not forget this one thing, that with the Lord one day is as a thousand years, and a thousand years as one day.*
>
> 2 Peter 3:8

One of the purposes of the seven-day creation story was to prefigure the 7,000 years of human history. God is always working toward perfection. We know that in Hebrew, seven is the number of perfection.

Furthermore, God as much as told Isaiah that the creation story told the whole story:

> *[9]Remember the former things of old, For I am God, and there is no other; I am God, and there is none like Me,*
> *[10]**Declaring the end from the beginning**...*
>
> Isaiah 46:9-10 (emphasis added)

Yahweh said something very similar through King Solomon, the wisest man who ever lived:

> *[9]**That which has been is what will be**, That which is done is what will be done, And there is nothing new under the sun.*
> *[10]Is there anything of which it may be said, "See, this is new?" **It has already been in ancient times before us.***
>
> Ecclesiastes 1:9-10 (emphasis added)

19

Let me use an example to illustrate this point. The first Jewish war, recorded in Genesis 14, has Abram the Hebrew battling the kings of Babylon (Shinar) and Persia. The final Jewish war, Armageddon, has Jesus, the King of the Jews again battling, and defeating antichrist, the King of Babylon (Jeremiah 25:26; Isaiah 14:4).

Thus we have events in the Bible playing out, all the while prefiguring future events, which God desires us to delve in to and understand.

This chart illustrates what we refer to as **God's Divine Week**.

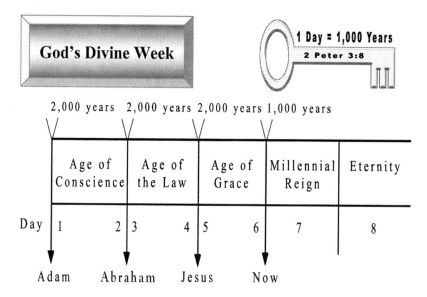

Using this chart, we see a total of seven days, which we understand from 2 Peter 3:8 to be seven thousand years. Adam was created at the beginning of day one, and after the fall of man was to find God's will by using his conscience. Thus, we have the first two thousand year period called the "Age of Conscience." Unfortunately, man did not do a very good job of living by his conscience, because seventeen hundred years into human history God, who is love, sent the flood.

Love sent the flood? Yes, dear reader, for you and I would not be here today if God had not sent the flood. Mankind was deteriorating into sinfulness so rapidly that soon all men would have been hell bound. In Genesis 11, right after the flood, we see Nimrod building the Tower of Babel, again defying God. God had to do something! And so, five generations later He raised up Abraham and gave man a better way to righteousness.

The "Age of the Law" began when God cut covenant with Abraham in Genesis 15. On Mount Sinai, the Law came into fullness when Moses was given the Ten Commandments. The "Age of the Law" was fulfilled with the ministry of the Lord Jesus, who was born in 3 B.C.

The "Age of Grace" was introduced at the Last Supper:

> *[26]And as they were eating, Jesus took bread, blessed and broke it, and gave it to the disciples and said, "Take, eat; this is My body."*
> *[27]Then he took the cup, and gave thanks, and gave it to them, saying, "Drink from it, all of you.*
> *[28]For this is My blood of **the new covenant**, which is shed for many for the remission of sins."*
> Matthew 26:26-28 (emphasis added)

It came into fullness on Pentecost Sunday:

> *[1]When the Day of Pentecost had fully come, they were all with one accord in one place.*
> *[2]And suddenly there came a sound from heaven, as of a rushing mighty wind, and it filled the whole house where they were sitting.*
> *[3]Then there appeared to them divided tongues, as of fire, and one sat upon each of them.*
> *[4]And they were **all filled with the Holy Spirit** and began to speak with other tongues, as the Spirit gave them utterance.*
> Acts 2:1-4 (emphasis added)

Today we are at the culmination of the "Age of Grace," also called the "Age of Faith" or the "Church Age."

We recall that when Moses came down the mountain with the Ten Commandments, he found the people in sin. As retribution, God required him to send the Levites among the people, executing **about three thousand** of them (Exodus 32:26-28). On Pentecost Sunday, the birth of the "Age of Grace," we see that **about three thousand** souls were added to the Church (Acts 2:41). Thus we see a great truth revealed: *"The letter kills but the Spirit gives life"* (2 Corinthians 3:6).

We should be forever grateful to the Lord for allowing us to live during the "Age of Grace." In the Bible, the "Age of Grace" is also referred to as the "Last Days." The Jews always referred to days by their number, in Biblical times. Sunday was "the first day of the week," Wednesday was the "fourth day of the week," etc. God always works toward perfection, and seven is the number of perfection. Thus, the Jews were always working toward the seventh day, the Sabbath, after which they would begin again.

Reviewing our chart, we see that the last two days (or 2,000 years) before the 1,000 year Sabbath rest, are days five and six. Hence, the following scriptures refer to the "Church Age" as the "Last Days."

> *[16]But this is what was spoken by the prophet Joel:*
> *[17]"And it shall come to pass in the last days, says God, That I will pour out of My Spirit on all flesh;"*
> Acts 2:16-17 (emphasis added)

> *[1]But know this, that in the last days perilous times will come:*
> *[2]For men will be lovers of themselves, lovers of money, boasters, proud, blasphemers, disobedient to parents, unthankful, unholy,...*
> 2 Timothy 3:1-2 (emphasis added)

> *[17]But you, beloved, remember the words which were spoken before by the apostles of our Lord Jesus Christ:*
> *[18]how they told you that there would be mockers in the last time who would walk according to their own ungodly lusts.*
> Jude 17-18 (emphasis added)

We are actually living at the end of the sixth, or last day. Some may ask, the last day before what? The answer is obvious: the last day before the Sabbath, or seventh day, the Millennial Age. Knowing that we are in the last day makes these words of Jesus in John so much clearer. He's telling us when the rapture will be. We are not surprised to find out we'll be raptured on the last day:

> *[40]And this is the will of Him who sent Me, that everyone who sees the Son and believes in Him may have everlasting life; and **I will raise him up at the last day**.*

> *[44]No one can come to Me unless the Father who sent Me draws him; and **I will raise him up at the last day**.*

> *[54]Whoever eats My flesh and drinks My blood has eternal life, and **I will raise him up at the last day**.*
>
> John 6:40, 44, 54 (emphasis added)

Sometimes the words "Last Days" and "End Times" are used interchangeably, but that is incorrect. The "Last Days" began, as I have illustrated, on Pentecost. The "End Times" began, in my opinion, when the Lord's parable of the fig tree (Israel) was fulfilled and Israel became a nation again, May 14, 1948.

> *[29]...Look at the fig tree, (Israel) and all the trees (nations of prophecy).*
> *[30]When they are already budding, (vibrant after 1900 years of dormancy), you see and know for yourselves that summer (the judgment of the nations) is now near.*
> *[31]So you also, when you see these things happening, (prophecy being fulfilled), know that the kingdom of God is near.*
> *[32]Assuredly, I say to you, this generation (alive in 1948) will by no means pass away till all these things take place."*
>
> Luke 21:29-32
> (parenthesis are author's interpretation)

23

The "End Times" will culminate in a period often referred to as "The Judgment of the Nations." Could it be that we are already in the time period known as "The Judgment of the Nations?" If so, what does the future hold for you and me?

CHAPTER 2
FTH

The Judgment of the Nations

The Judgment of the Nations is a time in history when nations will finally reap what they have sown. I recall giving certain counsel to my children many times as they were growing up: "No one ever gets away with anything." So it is also with the nations. In the last analysis, all judgment on this earth will be reduced to this question, "How did you treat Israel and the Jews?" (Matthew 25:31-46).

Many Christian and Jewish scholars believe the Judgment of the Nations began on Rosh Hashanah in the year right after 1998, the Year of the Jubilee. That is, the Judgment of the Nations began on September 11, 1999.[3]

If this is accurate, it could explain why satan chose September 11, 2001 as the date to attack the Twin Towers in New York, sort of a return salvo.

In any event, I believe we are living in that judgment time, which is characterized by:

All previously unfulfilled prophetic wars will occur. These wars include:

> The Iraqi War - Jeremiah 50, 51
> The leveling of Damascus - Isaiah 17
> The war of Gog and Magog – Ezekiel 38, 39
> Armageddon – Revelation 19:11-21 and Zechariah 12 & 14

This knowledge **should not strike terror** in the heart of the reader, just the opposite, really. We are living in the most exciting time of history, living in the greatest nation, with an unparalleled opportunity before us. We are not here by accident. God put us here at this time because He knew that by His grace we would get the job done! What job? The job of harvesting the seed sown by the sacrifice of the martyrs, the tears of the missionaries and the prayers of mothers and fathers on their knees for the past two thousand years! If we will stay faithful to our call, and most of us will, we will *"shine like the brightness of the firmament... and the stars forever and ever"* (Daniel 12:3).

Judgments will become more rapid in succession, and more severe.

> *[7]For nation will rise against nation, and kingdom against kingdom. And there will be famines, pestilences, and earthquakes in various places.*
>
> Matthew 24:7

God, who is love, will use these catastrophes and judgments to draw men to Himself.

> *[9]...For when Your judgments are in the earth, The inhabitants of the world will learn righteousness.*
>
> Isaiah 26:9

He will increase His glory during judgment.

> *[21]I will set My glory among the nations; all the nations shall see My judgment which I have executed, and My hand which I have laid on them.*
>
> Ezekiel 39:21

The time will finally come when the sin-laden nations will be weary and the glory will be full:

> *[13]Behold, is it not of the Lord of hosts That the peoples labor to feed the fire, And nations weary themselves in vain?*
> *[14]For the earth will be filled With the knowledge of the glory of the Lord, As the waters cover the sea.*
>
> Habakkuk 2:13-14

Then the Bride of Christ, the Church, will be raptured, as prophesied by Hosea: (remember that the Age of Grace lasts two thousand years, or "two days").

> *²After two days He will revive us; On the third day*
> *He will raise us up, That we may live in His sight.*
> Hosea 6:2

After the rapture, Jesus will receive us, the Bride of Christ, at the heavenly wedding feast. We see a confirmation of the timing of this wedding feast cleverly woven into the fabric of the gospel of John:

> *¹On the third day, there was a wedding...*
> John 2:1

This refers to the third day (1,000 years) of Christianity.

As we stated above, God always desires man to repent. Notice that even during the second half of the Tribulation, God sends angels to be seen by men, with warnings not to be ignored.

> *⁶Then I saw another angel flying in the midst of*
> *heaven, having the everlasting gospel to preach*
> *to those who dwell on the earth—to every nation,*
> *tribe, tongue, and people—*
> *⁷saying with a loud voice, "Fear God and give glory*
> *to Him, for the hour of His judgment has come;*
> *and worship Him who made heaven and earth,*
> *the sea and springs of water."*
> *⁹Then a third angel followed them, saying with a*
> *loud voice, **"If anyone worships the beast and***
> ***his image, and receives his mark on his forehead***
> ***or on his hand,***
> *¹⁰he himself shall also drink of the wine of the wrath*
> *of God, which is poured out full strength into the*
> *cup of His indignation. He shall be tormented with*
> *fire and brimstone in the presence of the holy*
> *angels and in the presence of the Lamb."*
> Revelation 14:6-7, 9-10 (emphasis added)

And finally, right before the battle of Armageddon, the Lord Himself, filled with love for His rebellious children, makes one last appeal:

> [15]*Behold, I am coming as a thief. Blessed is he who watches, and keeps his garments, lest he walk naked and they see his shame.*
> [16]*And they gathered them together to the place called in Hebrew, Armageddon.*
>
> Revelation 16:15-16

A review of the characteristics of the time of the Judgment of the Nations reveals: all Biblical wars will be completed, judgments will be progressively harsher and more proximate, and God's hand of mercy will be extended throughout.

As on earth, a court must be assembled in heaven, with a presiding judge, before a judgment can be pronounced. The world will have its day in court, as illustrated in both the Old and New Testaments:

> [9]*I beheld till the thrones were cast down, and the Ancient of days did sit, whose garment was white as snow, and the hair of his head like the pure wool: his throne was like the fiery flame, and his wheels as burning fire.*
> [10]*A fiery stream issued and came forth from before him: thousand thousands ministered unto him; and ten thousand times ten thousand stood before him: the judgment was set, and the books were opened.*
>
> Daniel 7:9-10 (KJV)

> [2]*Immediately I was in the Spirit; and behold, a throne set in heaven, and One sat on the throne.*
>
> [4]*Around the throne were twenty-four thrones, and on the thrones I saw twenty-four elders sitting, clothed in white robes and they had crowns of gold on their heads.*
>
> Revelation 4: 2, 4

> [7]*Then He came and took the book out of the right hand of Him who sat on the throne...*
> [11]*Then I looked, and I heard the voice of many angels around the throne, the living creatures, and the*

> *elders; and the number of them was ten thousand*
> *times ten thousand, and thousands of thousands.*
>
> Revelation 5:7, 11

Let us look again at the King James Version of Daniel 7:10:

> [10]*...the judgment was set, and the books were*
> *opened.*

As I have already pointed out, I believe the judgment was set on September 11, 1999 (see page 25). In the Bible, a punctuation mark can represent an extended period of time. I believe that we are living in a time represented by the comma after the word "set." We will continue in this time frame until after the rapture of the Church. At that time, the *"books will be opened." "And the books were opened"* is discussed in greater detail in Chapter 4.

The chart on the next page gives an analysis of what I believe will transpire during the time of the Judgment of the Nations. There is no unanimity of opinion among Bible teachers on the sequence of the events. I invite the readers to search the Scripture and see what the Holy Spirit reveals to their own hearts.

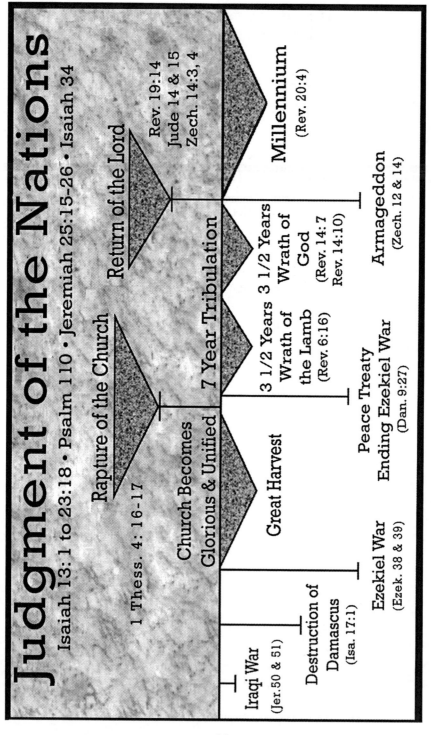

Judgment of the Nations
Isaiah 13: 1 to 23:18 • Psalm 110 • Jeremiah 25:15-26 • Isaiah 34

Iraqi War
(Jer.50 & 51)

Destruction of
Damascus
(Isa. 17:1)

Ezekiel War
(Ezek. 38 & 39)

Great Harvest

Church Becomes
Glorious & Unified

Rapture of the Church

1 Thess. 4: 16-17

Peace Treaty
Ending Ezekiel War
(Dan. 9:27)

7 Year Tribulation

3 1/2 Years
Wrath of
the Lamb
(Rev. 6:16)

3 1/2 Years
Wrath of
God
(Rev. 14:7
Rev. 14:10)

Armageddon
(Zech. 12 & 14)

Return of the Lord

Rev. 19:14
Jude 14 & 15
Zech. 14:3, 4

Millennium
(Rev. 20:4)

30

Some scholars believe the leveling of Damascus will be the event that triggers the war of Ezekiel 38 and 39. I agree with that view for four reasons:

1) Syria, an arch foe of Israel, does not take part in the attack against Israel in Ezekiel 38 and 39.

2) Two powerful eschatological portions of Scripture, the book of Amos and Zechariah: Chapter 9, begin with the destruction of Damascus.

3) Isaiah 17, the Chapter that prophesies *"Damascus will cease from being a city,"* ends with three verses (12-14) that appear to be the Ezekiel war. This would imply that the destruction of Damascus precedes the Ezekiel war.

> *[12]Woe to the multitude of many people Who make a noise like the roar of the seas, And to the rushing of nations That make a rushing like the rushing of mighty waters!*
>
> *[13]The nations will rush like the rushing of many waters; But God will rebuke them and they will flee far away, And be chased like the chaff of the mountains before the wind, Like a rolling thing before the whirlwind.*
>
> *[14]Then behold, at eventide, trouble! And before the morning, he is no more. This is the portion of those who plunder us, And the lot of those who rob us.*
>
> Isaiah 17:12-14

4) Building on what I have just explained, a careful reading of Jeremiah 49:23-27 seems to prophesy a naval attack by the Israelis leading to a fire in Damascus, no doubt a very powerful bomb. (Amos 1:4 confirms that fire will devour Damascus) I have emphasized verse 25. We see the prophet Jeremiah implying this in verse 25: The Syrians are attacking us. We must either destroy Damascus or evacuate Jerusalem. We choose, therefore, to destroy Damascus. (Jerusalem, of course is the city of God's joy.)

> *shamed, For they have heard bad news. They are*
> *fainthearted; There is trouble on the sea; It cannot*
> *be quiet.*
> *[24]Damascus has grown feeble; She turns to flee. And*
> *fear has seized her. Anguish and sorrows have*
> *taken her like a woman in labor.*
> *[25]**Why is the city of praise not deserted, the city of***
> ***My joy?***
> *[26]Therefore her young men shall fall in her streets,*
> *And all the men of war shall be cut off in that day,"*
> *says the Lord of hosts.*
> *[27]"I will kindle a fire in the wall of Damascus, And*
> *it shall consume the palaces of Ben-Hadad."*
> Jeremiah 49:23-27 (emphasis added)

I will discuss the Ezekiel war in detail in Chapter 6. It is pivotal to understanding the direction to which each of the four horsemen will travel.

The first of the four horsemen, the man on the white horse, we believe will be the antichrist. As one of the most enigmatic persons in Biblical prophecy much has been written about him.

I will not name a particular person. I believe it is very insulting and presumptuous to accuse someone of being the antichrist.

Furthermore, Scripture teaches that he will be revealed after the rapture.

> *[7]For the mystery of lawlessness is already at work;*
> *only He who now restrains will do so until He is*
> *taken out of the way.*
> *[8]And then the lawless one will be revealed, whom*
> *the Lord will consume with the breath of His mouth*
> *and destroy with the brightness of His coming.*
> 2 Thessalonians 2:7-8

Who is "He" who restrains the antichrist, forbidding him from being revealed? He is the Body of Christ. Now we know that the Body of Christ is sometimes referred to in the feminine as the "Bride of Christ." The Body of Christ is also referred to sometimes in the masculine:

32

> *[13]till we all come to the unity of the faith and of the knowledge of the Son of God, to a **perfect man**, to the measure of the stature of the fullness of Christ;*
> Ephesians 4:13 (emphasis added)

Therefore, "He" who restrains the antichrist from being revealed is none other than the "perfect man" of Ephesians 4:13. Namely, "He" is the Body of Christ.

Let me outline a series of events, which I believe will soon transpire on the earth.

1) Syria will attack Israel.
2) Israel will counterattack by sea to save Jerusalem, leveling Damascus.
3) Indignation in Russia and the Moslem community will precipitate the Ezekiel War.
4) God will defeat the Russian and Moslem invaders on the mountains of Israel (see Chapter 6).
5) A diplomat will come from Syria to Jerusalem to broker a seven year peace treaty with Israel. This diplomat is the antichrist:

> *[27]Then he shall confirm a covenant with many for one week; But in the middle of the week he shall bring an end to sacrifice and offering. And on the wing of abominations shall be one who makes desolate, Even until the consummation, which is determined, Is poured out on the desolate.*
> Daniel 9:27

Let us read on to see what else the Scripture has to say about this diabolical man.

CHAPTER
3
FTH

The Antichrist Persona

Before I attempt to identify the four horsemen, we must understand where the antichrist comes from, since he rides on one of the horses. He is identified in Revelation 13:1 as a beast with seven heads. Those seven heads represent the kingdoms that have come against national Israel throughout history (see chart below).

The vision of the four beasts in Daniel 7 identifies the four world powers that dominated ancient Jerusalem, described as beasts.

Seven kingdoms against national Israel:

Egypt Assyria	**Daniel 7:4-8** **"Four Great Beasts"**
Babylon..........................Lion Medo-Persia.................Bear Greece...........................Leopard Rome............................Dreadful Beast	
Revived Rome	

A comparison of the beasts in Daniel 7:4-8 and the description of antichrist in Revelation is striking:

> *²Now the beast which I saw was like a **leopard**, his feet were like the feet of a **bear**, and his mouth like the mouth of a **lion**. The dragon gave him his power, his throne, and great authority.*
>
> Revelation 13:2 (emphasis added)

I render this description to infer: Now the antichrist was like a Greek (**leopard**), his feet walked where the Medo-Persians (**bear**) walked, and his mouth devoured what the Babylonians (**lion**) devoured.

Thus I conclude that the antichrist will be of Greek origin, take over Iraq as the Medo-Persians did and subsequently "devour" Jerusalem as the Babylonians did. In fact, the antichrist is referred to as the King of Babylon (Isaiah 14:4) and the King of Sheshach (Jeremiah 25:26). Sheshach is a code name for Babylon. The antichrist is also called the Assyrian (Isaiah 10:24 and 14:25 and Micah 5:5,6). Therefore, the antichrist must be from Assyria and someday reign as King of Babylon to fulfill scripture.

In Daniel we see the antichrist introduced as the "little horn," that comes out of the ten horns, or ten kingdoms of the end times.

> *⁷After this I saw in the night visions, and behold, a fourth beast, dreadful and terrible, exceedingly strong. It had huge iron teeth; it was devouring, breaking in pieces, and trampling the residue with its feet. It was different from all the beasts that were before it, and it had ten horns.*
>
> *⁸I was considering the horns, and there was **another horn, a little one**, coming up among them, before whom three of the first horns were plucked out by the roots. And there, in this horn, are eyes like the eyes of a man, and a mouth speaking pompous words.*
>
> Daniel 7:7-8 (emphasis added)

We don't have to try to interpret these verses, since someone who saw the vision with Daniel, probably an angel, gives the interpretation.

> *[23]The fourth beast shall be a fourth kingdom on earth, which shall be different from all other kingdoms, and shall devour the whole earth, trample it and break it in pieces.*
>
> *[24]The ten horns are ten kings who shall arise from this kingdom. And **another shall rise after them; he shall be different from the first ones, and shall subdue three kings**.*
>
> *[25]He shall speak pompous words against the Most High, shall persecute the saints of the Most High, and shall intend to change times and law. Then the saints shall be given into his hand for a time and times and half a time.*
>
> Daniel 7:23-25 (emphasis added)

Agreeing with Daniel 7:24, Daniel Chapter 8 narrows down the focus of who the little horn could be:

> *[8]Therefore the male goat grew very great; but when he became strong, the large horn was broken, and in place of it four notable ones came up toward the four winds of heaven.*
>
> *[9]**And out of one of them came a little horn,** which grew exceedingly great toward the south, toward the east, and toward the Glorious Land.*
>
> Daniel 8:8-9 (emphasis added)

We are grateful to the Angel Gabriel, who interpreted the vision for Daniel.

> *[21]And the male goat is the kingdom of Greece. The large horn that is between its eyes is the first king.*
>
> *[22]As for the broken horn and the four that stood up in its place, four kingdoms shall arise out of that nation, but not with its power.*
>
> *[23]And **in the latter time of their kingdom, when the transgressors have reached their fullness, a king shall arise**, having fierce features, who understands sinister schemes.*

> [24]*His power shall be mighty, but not by his own power; He shall destroy fearfully, and shall prosper and thrive; He shall destroy the mighty, and also the holy people.*
>
> Daniel 8:21-24 (emphasis added)

Thus, we see that the little horn, the antichrist, must arise out of one of the four divisions of Alexander's Greek empire.

A careful rendering of ancient Greek history shows that the "first king," Alexander the Great, died in 323 B.C. At that time, his kingdom was divided between four generals. They are the four kingdoms referred to in Daniel 8:22.

General		Geographical Area
General Cassander	took	Greece
General Lysimachus	took	Turkey
General Seleucus	took	Syria & Iraq
General Ptolemy	took	Egypt

The next verse, Daniel 8:23, makes it clear that the antichrist will arise from one of these four kingdoms. It's important to note that all four generals were Greek by nationality, as stated in Daniel 8:22 (remember the antichrist must be of Greek national origin to satisfy Revelation 13:2).

Antichrist is also called the "Assyrian" and the "King of Babylon." So let us take a closer look at General Seleucus, who ruled out of Antioch, Syria. Assyria included Syria, Lebanon, part of Turkey, Iran and Iraq; the borders were very fluid. Babylon conquered Assyria in 612 B.C. The combination of Babylon and Assyria is known as the "Fertile Crescent."

It is believed by many that the "Fertile Crescent" will be the power base of the future antichrist. Political events that are causing such havoc in the Middle East because of the Iraqi War make it seem plausible that Iraq and Syria may form some type of alliance. If that happens it would cause an Assyrian to also become the "King of Babylon" in the near future. Another title given the antichrist in Daniel 11 is "King of the North."

It appears we are looking for a man of Greek national origin, whose citizenship is in Syria, and will be called the "King of the North," who will one day seize Jerusalem as his base, and set an idol in the holy place. Has there ever been such an evil person on the face of the earth? The answer is "yes," the Seleucid king, Antiochus IV Epiphanes. King Antiochus Epiphanes was a ruthless Greek ruler from Syria who was determined to totally subjugate Jewish culture. Greek language and customs were thrust upon the Jews, and worship of Zeus, the Greek god was mandated. Antiochus IV ruled from 175 B.C. to 164 B.C. Fierce resistance by the Jews, rallied by a great warrior named Judas Maccabee, characterized the last three years of his reign. Jewish scholars see the Jewish military victory over Antiochus Epiphanes in 164 B.C. as a fulfillment of this prophecy written three hundred years before the war.

> *[13]For I have bent Judah, My bow, fitted the bow with Ephraim, And raised up your sons, O Zion, Against your sons, O Greece, And made you like the sword of a mighty man.*
>
> Zechariah 9:13

However, David Baron states emphatically "the prophecy cannot be altogether restricted to the Maccabean struggle with the Syrian Greeks."[4] David Baron was born in Russia in 1855 and raised in the best Rabbinical schools of Europe. He found Jesus to be Messiah while studying the Old Testament. His prolific writings were addressed to Jews and Christians alike. He goes on to explain:

```
No; Zion and Greece, as has been
well observed by another writer,
are in this prophecy of Zechariah
opposed to one another as the city
of God and the city of the world
```

(the civitas Dei, and the civitas
mundi, as Augustine has it), and
the defeat of Antiochus Epiphanes
and his successors at the hands of
comparative handfuls of despised
Jews, to which this passage may
primarily refer, **foreshadows the
final conflict with world-power, and
the judgments to be inflicted on
the confederated armies who shall
be gathered against Jerusalem,** not
only directly by the hand of God,
but also by the hand of Israel, who
shall then be made strong in
Jehovah.[5] (emphasis added)

Thus we see the defeat of Antiochus Epiphanes by Judas
Maccabee prefigures the defeat of antichrist by the Lord Jesus
Christ.

The comparison in the chart on the next page between
Antiochus Epiphanes and the coming antichrist includes many
chilling facts:

		ANTIOCHUS	ANTICHRIST
1.	Called the "little horn."	Daniel 8:9	Daniel 7:8
2a.	Outlaws the solemn feasts.	2 Maccabees 6:6	-------------------
2b.	Attempts to outlaw the feasts.	-------------------	Daniel 7:25
3.	Takes away daily sacrifice.	Daniel 8:11	Daniel 9:27
4.	Defiles the temple of God.	2 Maccabees 6:1	Daniel 9:27
5a.	Compels the people to worship the god Bacchus or be put to death.	2 Maccabees 6:7-9	-------------------
5b.	Compels the people to worship the beast, his image, or be put to death.	-------------------	Revelation 13:15-17
6.	Jews will suffer under his reign but not be forsaken by God.	2 Maccabees 6:16	Daniel 2:44 Daniel 7:25-26
7.	Sets up the idol of abomination of desolation on the altar of God.	1 Maccabees 1:57	Mark 13:14
8.	Called the "King of the North."	Daniel 11:6	Daniel 11:40
9.	Attacks & defeats Egypt	Daniel 11:11-15	Daniel 11:40
10.	An extended peace follows his overthrow.	Peace from 163 B.C. to 63 B.C.	Revelation 20:4 (Jesus reigns for 1,000 years)

One of the notable differences between Antiochus Epiphanes and the antichrist has to do with religious beliefs. Antiochus Epiphanes was a pagan, while the antichrist will worship a *"god of forces"* (Daniel 11:38). Islam has always conquered by military force. Many modern scholars believe antichrist will be a Moslem military leader.

The Shiite Moslem doctrine of the "Mahdi" (the holy one) teaches that the twelfth prophet (descendant of Ali) disappeared in the desert in the 800's. He is allegedly a "sinless and absolutely infallible" holy man who will come back from the desert at the end of the age and lead the world into a totally Moslem society.[6]

It is interesting to note that the Shiite branch of the Islamic faith is on the rise, particularly among the young and impoverished in Moslem countries. Mohammad's command to his followers before his death was: "Fight until all declare, there is no god but Allah."

Could that command be the driving force behind the war of terror that is currently being waged against us?

Before we leave the antichrist model, let us refer the reader back to #7 in the chart on page 41. We will examine the term "abomination of desolation" in light of the Book of Maccabees. (Maccabees are considered historical, but not part of Scripture, except by the Catholic Church.)

Daniel warns of the abomination of desolation:

> *[11]And from the time that the daily sacrifice is taken away, and the abomination of desolation is set up, there shall be one thousand two hundred and ninety days.*
>
> Daniel 12:11

Jesus affirms the accuracy of Daniel's prophecy in Mark 13:14: *"So when you see the 'abomination of desolation,' spoken of by Daniel the prophet, standing where it ought not"* — (let the reader understand) — *"then let those who are in Judea flee to the mountains."* And so we ask the question, what is the *"abomination of desolation?"* In the light of the Book of Maccabees, we understand that they are referring to an idol called in the Book of Revelation the *"image of the beast."* King Antiochus set up as an idol, a statue of Jupiter, on the altar:

> *[57]On the fifteenth day of the month Casleu, the hundred and forty-fifth year, king Antiochus set up the abominable idol of desolation upon the altar of God,...*
>
> I Maccabees 1: 57

We know from the Word of God that the false prophet will set up an image of the beast.

> *[14]And he deceives those who dwell on the earth by those signs which he was granted to do in the sight*

of the beast, telling those who dwell on the earth to make an image to the beast who was wounded by the sword and lived.
*[15]He was granted power to give breath to the image of the beast, that the image of the beast should both speak and **cause as many as would not worship the image of the beast to be killed**.*

Revelation 13:14-15 (emphasis added)

In conclusion let us re-examine two important facts:

1) The Moslems are waiting for a world leader to come out of the desert and take over the world.
2) Half way through the Tribulation Period, (Daniel 9:27), antichrist will set up the image of the beast inside the Temple Holy Place. Consider the warning of Jesus to those who will be alive during the Tribulation Period, in light of these two facts:

[25] See, I have told you beforehand.
*[26]Therefore if they say to you, "Look, **He is in the desert!**" do not go out; or "Look, **He is in the inner rooms!**" Do not believe it.*

Matthew 24:25-26 (emphasis added)

It is quite possible that the Lord is referring in this scripture to the Moslem world leader, *"He is in the desert,"* and the image of the beast, *"He is in the inner rooms"* (we will look at the beast and his image in greater detail in Chapter 13).

As I stated in Chapter 2 of this book, the Judgment of the Nations has already begun. What is the one thing holding back the four horsemen of the Apocalypse? The books have not been opened.

[10]...the judgment was set, and the books were opened.

Daniel 7:10 (KJV)

When the books are opened, the four horsemen will be released. But who will open the books?

CHAPTER

4

FTH

The Four Horsemen Defined

The entire 5th Chapter of the Book of Revelation is the story of who will open the book. (Although the New King James Version calls it a scroll, that is incorrect. "Scroll" is a correct translation of Revelation 6:14, but not a correct translation of the book in Revelation Chapter 5. Strong's Concordance calls the "book" *biblion*, the diminutive of *biblos*, from which we get the word Bible.) A frantic search is made in heaven, then on earth, and finally, even in hell to find someone who is worthy to open the book (Revelation 5:3). No one is found. John feels so helpless, he weeps much (Revelation 5:4). Why would John weep? Because he sees the Judgment of the Nations has begun. He knows the book must be opened, in order to conclude the time of judgment. After the judgment, the Messiah will come, and John's beloved country, Israel, will be returned to its rightful place. It will be the center of all earthly business, the ruling kingdom of the world. The Temple will be rebuilt, and there will be heaven on earth. Like any good Jew, he longs for this day.

Suddenly, standing before him, is "the Lamb that was slain." What joy! What ecstasy! Worship and praise follow. And then Jesus walks up to His Father, takes the book, and begins to break the seals.

Thus, the book is opened. Revelation Chapter 6 reveals that when the first four seals of the book are broken by Jesus, riders come riding on horses: white, red, black and green. The King James Version of the Bible refers to the fourth horse as the pale horse. However, the actual word in Greek translates as green. Much speculation has gone forth throughout the ages on this topic. Who are those riders, where are they going, and for what purpose? As stated in the Prologue of this book, *"It is also written in your law that the testimony of two men is true,"* John 8:17. Surely, if we search the scriptures, we will find the four horses somewhere else besides the Book of Revelation. Knowing that the three great pieces of the "end times puzzle" are the books of Daniel, Zechariah and Revelation, we expect to find four horsemen in one of those books, and we are not disappointed.

Who are those riders and where are they going?

Indeed, in Zechariah we find four horses in Chapter 1, and four chariots in Chapter 6. The book of Zechariah was written soon after the Jews returned to Israel from the seventy-year exile in Babylon, a punishment God had sent because of their disobedience and idol worship. Zechariah Chapters 1 through 6 contain a series of eight visions the prophet had in one night, which portray a "connected picture of the future of Israel linked on to the then existing time, and closing with the prospect of the ultimate completion of the Kingdom of God." [7]

Let us now consider the four horses of Zechariah Chapter 1:

> [8]*I saw by night, and behold, a man riding on a red horse, and it stood among the myrtle trees in the hollow; and behind him were horses: red, sorrel, and white.*
>
> [9]*Then I said, "My lord, what are these?" So the angel who talked with me said to me, "I will show you what they are."*
>
> [10]*And the man who stood among the myrtle trees answered and said, "These are the ones whom the Lord has sent to walk to and fro throughout the earth."*
>
> [11]*So they answered the Angel of the Lord, who stood among the myrtle trees, and said, "We have walked*

> *to and fro throughout the earth, and behold, all
> the earth is resting quietly."*
> [12]*Then the Angel of the Lord answered and said,
> "O Lord of hosts, how long will You not have
> mercy on Jerusalem and on the cities of Judah,
> against which You were angry these seventy
> years?"*
>
> Zechariah 1:8-12

In my judgment, **these horses could not be the horses of the Apocalypse** for several reasons:

1) There are two red horses, and Revelation Chapter 6 has only one red horse.
2) The man riding on a red horse in verse 8 is identified in verse 11 as the Angel of the Lord. **"He is 'the Angel of Jehovah,' who is none other than the 'Angel of His face,' the Divine 'Angel of the Covenant,' the second person in the Blessed Trinity."** [8] Jesus could not be riding one of the horses, since He is in heaven breaking the seals.
3) Verse 12 puts the time of this vision as immediately following the Babylonian exile, approximately 520 B.C. The four horsemen will not go forth until the end of the age, probably very soon.

As I have indicated, the eight visions are sequential, as to time, and the eighth vision occurs right before dawn. Therefore, the vision of the four chariots, the final vision, would appear to fit chronologically during these end times. **The four chariots appear to be our introduction to the four horsemen.**

Let us now examine the vision of the four chariots of Zechariah: Chapter 6.

> [1]*Then I turned and raised my eyes and looked, and
> behold, four chariots were coming from between
> two mountains, and the mountains were mountains
> of bronze.*
> [2]*With the first chariot were red horses, with the*

second chariot black horses,

³with the third chariot white horses, and with the fourth chariot dappled horses—strong steeds.

⁴Then I answered and said to the angel who talked with me, "What are these, my lord?"

⁵And the angel answered and said to me, "These are four spirits of heaven, who go out from their station before the Lord of all the earth."

⁶"The one with the black horses is going to the north country, the white are going after them, and the dappled are going toward the south country."

⁷Then the strong steeds went out, eager to go, that they might walk to and fro throughout the earth. And He said, "Go, walk to and fro throughout the earth." So they walked to and fro throughout the earth.

⁸And He called to me, and spoke to me, saying, "See, those who go toward the north country have given rest to My Spirit in the north country."

Zechariah 6:1-8

Much debate has centered around the words of verse seven, namely who are the "strong steeds?" Since the black, white and dappled horses are enumerated in verse six, I believe the "strong steeds" of verse seven are the red ones. In both Zechariah and Revelation, only the red horses go to the whole earth.

Furthermore, I agree with David Baron's translation of verse eight to be correct, as we note that "ruach," translated in the King James as "Spirit" can also be translated "anger." Thus the eighth verse should read instead as: *"See, those who go to the north country have caused my anger to rest on the north country."* (Zechariah 6:8) **"The meaning of the 8ᵗʰ verse, then, is that that company of invisible host whose mission was toward the north country caused God's anger to rest on it."** [9] Therefore, when we compare the chariots of Zechariah Chapter 6 with the mission of the horsemen in Revelation Chapter 6, we will see the events which have caused God's anger to rest on the north country.

And so, as I have just indicated, I believe the four horses of

Revelation Chapter 6 are indeed another look at the four chariots of Zechariah Chapter 6. I hold this view for several reasons:

1) The horses of Zechariah's chariots are: red, black, white and dappled (i.e. spotted).
2) The horses of the Apocalypse are: red, black, white and green (pale in KJV). [The mystery of why the "dappled" horses, which I identify as Rome, are classified as green in the New Testament will be discussed in a later chapter.]
3) Chronologically, the four horsemen come on the scene at the beginning of the Tribulation Period. The Lord's return is then depicted seven years later in the Book of Revelation.

In the book of Zechariah, the four chariots are introduced in Zechariah 6:1-8.

Notice that the return of the Lord comes soon after their assignment is completed four verses later:

> *[12]...From His place He shall branch out, And He shall build the temple of the Lord;*
> *[13]Yes, He shall build the temple of the Lord. He shall bear the glory, And shall sit and rule on His throne; So He shall be a priest on His throne, And the counsel of peace shall be between them both.*
>   Zechariah 6:12-13

4) The four chariots are identified for us in Zechariah 6:5. They are "the four spirits of heaven, who go out from their station before the Lord of all the earth."

In order for my analogy to be accurate, the four horses of the Apocalypse must be good, i.e. "spirits of heaven." A careful reading of the text in Revelation, Chapter 6 indicates that **it is the riders who cause such calamity to come upon the earth. The horses are God's agents who facilitate the judgments that are to come upon the earth.**

> *[1]Now I saw when the Lamb opened one of the seals; and I heard one of the four living creatures, saying*

with a voice like thunder, "Come and see."
*²And I looked, and behold, a white horse. He **who***
***sat on it had a bow**; and a crown was given to*
him, and he went out conquering and to conquer.
³When He opened the second seal, I heard the second
living creature saying, "Come and see."
*⁴Another horse, fiery red, went out, And **it was***
granted to the one who sat on it to take peace
***from the earth**, and that people should kill one*
another; and there was given to him a great sword.
⁵When He opened the third seal, I heard the third
living creature say, "Come and see." So I looked,
*and behold, a black horse, and **he who sat on it***
***had a pair of scales** in his hand.*
⁶And I heard a voice in the midst of the four living
creatures saying, "A quart of wheat for a denarius,
and three quarts of barley for a denarius; and do
not harm the oil and the wine."
⁷When He opened the fourth seal, I heard the voice
of the fourth living creature saying "Come and
see."
*⁸So I looked, and behold, a pale horse. **And the name***
***of him who sat on it was Death**, and Hades*
followed with him. And power was given to them
over a fourth of the earth, to kill with sword, with
hunger, with death, and by the beasts of the earth.
Revelation 6:1-8 (emphasis added)

Therefore, I believe the four horses are the same "four spirits of heaven" that go forth in the book of Zechariah. Notice that they are sent out by the four living creatures, also called the four "Cherubs" in the book of Ezekiel. With voices like thunder they give the command to "come," and the horses are released.

The four living creatures, whose assignment is to "send out" the horses, represent the four earthly directions upon which judgment must come. The world is described in the Bible as a giant cosmic house, complete with a cornerstone.

*⁴Where were you when I laid the foundations of the
earth? Tell Me, if you have understanding.*
*⁵Who determined its measurements? Surely you
know! Or who stretched the line upon it?*
*⁶To what were its foundations fastened? Or who laid
its cornerstone,*

Job 38:4-6

When the sixth seal is opened, cosmic disturbances shake the earth.

*¹²I looked when He opened the sixth seal, and
behold, there was a great earthquake and the sun
became black as sackcloth of hair, and the moon
became like blood.*
*¹³And the stars of heaven fell to the earth, as a fig
tree drops its late figs when it is shaken by a mighty
wind.*
*¹⁴Then the sky receded as a scroll when it is rolled
up, and every mountain and island was moved out
of its place.*

Revelation 6:12-14

Thus, we see a picture of judgment going throughout the earth, but in a limited way, during the time of the Wrath of the Lamb. A careful reading of the Book of Revelation indicates that there are two different three and a half year periods during the Tribulation. The first half is called the "Wrath of the Lamb," Revelation 6:16, and the second half, the "Wrath of God," Revelation 14:7. For our purpose in this chapter, it is important to see the assignment of the four horsemen is to bring judgment to the part of the earth that surrounds the Mediterranean Sea: Europe, the Middle East, Northern Africa, and also to Russia.

5) Finally, the matching of the four chariots of Zechariah with the four horsemen of Revelation, including the direction and purpose of their mission, works together "hand in glove." Zechariah tells us who they are and where they are going. Revelation tells us why.

So, who are they? Again, we trust David Baron to explain:

> The number four clearly brings to our mind again the four great Gentile world-powers whose successive course makes up "the times of the Gentiles," and whose final overthrow must precede the restoration and blessing of Israel, and the visible establishment of the Messianic Kingdom.[10]

> These four are the Babylonian, the Medo-Persian, the Grecian (or Graeco-Macedonian), and the Roman. "These are the horns (or Gentile powers) which have scattered Judah, Israel, and Jerusalem" (chap. I. 19), and it is the overthrow and judgment of these, by means of invisible heavenly powers appointed of God as a necessary precursor to the establishment of Messiah's kingdom, and the blessing of Israel, which is symbolically set forth to the prophet in this last vision.[11]

And so, the mystery is revealed. The first time the chariots are introduced is in Zechariah 6:2-3. They are in chronological order here. We take their identity from these verses.

Then in Zechariah 6:6-7 we see which direction they are going. This helps us greatly when we come to Revelation. For in Revelation Chapter 6 we have their missions explained.

Identity and Purpose of the Four Chariots/Horsemen

	Color	Country	Mission	Direction	Order of Appearance (In Revelation)
1st Chariot	RED	Babylon (Iraq)	Take a sword (Islam) throughout the earth	To the whole earth	Second
2nd Chariot	BLACK	Medo-Persia (Iran)	Famine and hunger in Iran, Russia, and all the countries that fought Israel in the Ezekiel war	North	Third
3rd Chariot	WHITE	Greece	The antichrist leaves Israel after the Peace Treaty of Dan. 9:27 and goes north to coalesce his base.	North	First
4th Chariot	DAPPLED /GREEN	Rome	Given power over ¼ of the earth (The early Roman empire also dominated ¼ of the earth) The evil twins, "Death and Hell," kill with war, hunger, beasts of the earth and their own evil spiritual power.	South	Fourth

The mission of each horseman will be examined more closely in Chapter 7. The conclusions drawn are based on a combination of:

1) What the scriptures say
2) What Bible teachers have taught
3) Current events
4) Our own interpretations

Thus, I readily admit that one could easily differ with my opinion. I invite the reader to study the scriptures and come up with other probable scenarios. My purpose is to stir in the heart of the reader, a sense of imminence, regarding the events about which I write.

A Dappled /Green Horse

As I have stated, the four world powers that are subject to judgment, according to Zechariah and Revelation are:

1) Babylon (Iraq)..Red Horse

2) Medo-Persia (Iran).......................................Black Horse

3) Greece..Whie Horse

4) Rome..Dappled/Green Horse

These are the ancient enemies and oppressors of God's chosen people.

In the Book of Daniel, these same four empires are first illustrated prophetically in Chapter 2, in Nebuchadnezzar's image.

1) Babylon	Head of gold	Daniel 2:32
2) Medo-Persia	Chest and arms of silver	Daniel 2:32
3) Greece	Belly and thighs of bronze	Daniel 2:32
4) Rome	Legs of iron	Daniel 2:33
5) Revived Rome	Feet of iron and clay	Daniel 2:41-43

Of the feet of iron and clay Daniel says:

> [41]*Whereas you saw the feet and toes, partly of potter's **clay and partly of iron**, the kingdom shall be divided; yet the strength of the iron shall be in it, just as you saw the iron mixed with the ceramic clay.*
> [42]*And as the toes of the feet were partly of iron and **partly of clay**, so the kingdom shall be partly strong and partly fragile.*
> [43]*As you saw **iron mixed with ceramic clay**, they will mingle with the seed of men; but they will not adhere to one another, just as iron does not mix with clay.*
>
> Daniel 2:41-43 (emphasis added)

Daniel repeats three times the vision of iron mixed with clay. It is possible the feet of the image had a spotted or "dappled" appearance. More than a hundred years later, when Zechariah wrote his book and called the horses of the fourth chariot "dappled," there must have been much curiosity about who this fourth and final kingdom would be. Clearly, from the prophets, the Jews could conclude it would be a strong and cruel empire.

By the time John wrote the book of Revelation on the island of Patmos, all Jews knew who the fourth kingdom was, because they were much oppressed by it. This fourth

Despised And Pagan Rome

kingdom was Rome, their conqueror, their subjugator—despised and pagan Rome.

John personally had much to fear from Rome. They had tried to boil him in oil, but he didn't die. So the emperor Domitian had him exiled to the island of Patmos.

Let us consider again the four chariots of Zechariah versus the four horses of the apocalypse. Refer to the chart on the next page:

Kingdom	Zechariah's Chariots	John's Horses
Babylon	Red	Red
Medo-Persia	Black	Black
Greece	White	White
Rome	Dappled	Green

Why does the color not match in the Roman horse? I believe that John knew, as did all the Jewish Christians of his era, that Zechariah and Daniel had prophesied severe judgment would befall the fourth kingdom, according to Scripture. **John could not risk his own life and the lives of fellow believers by linking Rome with the books of Zechariah and Daniel.** Therefore, I believe, either John or the Lord encoded Rome in a color that would not fit the pattern: *chloros*, in Greek, or green. (The King James incorrectly identifies the horse as pale. However, the word *chloros* is used to describe "green grass" in Revelation 8:7 and "neither any green thing" in Revelation 9:4. We get our word "chlorophyll" from this word.)

We observe that John also employed this same vehicle, encoding the name for Rome, in Revelation 17. We identify Rome in Revelation 17:9 as a city that sits on seven hills. Also, in Revelation 17:18 Rome is identified as "the great city that reigns over the kings of the earth." As previously discussed in this chapter, the "ten toes" of Daniel, Chapter 2, are the kings who reign in the revived Roman Empire. A careful reading of the 17th Chapter of Revelation reveals that John calls that city, which is actually Rome, "Mystery Babylon the Great" in verse five, and "the harlot" in verses 15 and 16. Again, I feel this was encoded to prevent the ire of the Romans from falling on the Jewish Christians (see Chapter 11).

The color of the Roman horse, green, will still have significance, of course. Never, in the entire Bible, is a word ever wasted or without meaning. Could it be that the green represents a radical left wing movement that is currently sweeping Europe? I am referring to the environmental movement, which hold that "Mother Earth" is sacred - namely, Greenpeace or the Green Party.

CHAPTER 6
FTH

World Conflict/World Harvest

When General Titus, the Roman warrior, surrounded and sacked Jerusalem in 70 A.D., the Jews were enslaved and taken to the four corners of the earth. It is a testament to God's faithfulness that they were never assimilated into the culture of any nation to which they were assigned. God had called the Jews to be a holy nation:

> *⁵Now therefore, if you will indeed obey My voice and keep My covenant, then you shall be a special treasure to Me above all people, for all the earth is Mine.*
> *⁶And you shall be to Me a kingdom of priests and a holy nation. These are the words which you shall speak to the children of Israel.*
> Exodus 19:5-6

The Jews were required to depart from the promised land three times:

1) During the famine in Jacob's day when they went to Egypt, where they were fed by their brother Joseph, whom God had sent ahead to preserve them
2) In 586 B.C. when King Nebuchadnezzar took them to Babylon for seventy years
3) In 70 A.D. when Titus the Roman dispersed them throughout the world

God had always promised them that their ultimate end would be to return to Israel, the center of the earth, to rule and reign with

Him forever.

> [14]*Also the sons of those who afflicted you shall come bowing to you, all those who despised you shall fall prostrate at the soles of your feet; And **they shall call you The City of the Lord, Zion of the Holy One of Israel.***
> [15]*Whereas you have been forsaken and hated, that no one went through you, I will make you an eternal excellence, joy of many generations.*
>
> Isaiah 60:14-15 (emphasis added)

> [2]*And behold, the glory of the God of Israel came from the way of the east. His voice was like the sound of many waters; and the earth shone with His glory.*
> [5]*The Spirit lifted me up and brought me into the inner court; and behold, the glory of the Lord filled the temple.*
> [6]*Then I heard Him speaking to me from the temple, while a man stood beside me.*
> [7]*And He said to me, "Son of man, this is the place of My throne and the place of the soles of My feet, **where I will dwell in the midst of the children of Israel forever...***"
>
> Ezekiel 43:2; 5-7 (emphasis added)

The nation of Israel was reborn on May 14, 1948. When the United Nations agreed to give the Jews their land back because they had suffered so in the holocaust, literal hell broke loose. Because Jesus Himself will rule and reign from Jerusalem, the devil has refused to allow the Jews to live in peace.

The wars the Jews have endured in modern times include:

1) 1948 – the war for independence
2) The 1956 War
3) 1967 – the Six Day War
4) 1973 – the Yom Kippur War
5) 2000 – the Intifada

The Intifada, or War of Terror, is ongoing as I write this book. The term "suicide bomber," or more accurately "homicide bomber," is a vehicle used by satan to destroy Jews and Arabs. Only God knows how many young Moslems have descended into hell for eternity, awakened to the stark reality that it was not God who encouraged them to commit murder.

The Bible clearly teaches that the devil will once again try to wrest the Holy Land from the grasp of the chosen people. A certain war, called the war of Gog and Magog, or the war of Ezekiel 38 and 39, even now is on the radar screen, as we look at current events.

Every country has been assigned a special angel to protect it by God. Likewise, satan has assigned to each country a "chief prince," to destroy it. The chief prince over Russia is a sinister being named "Gog." While no unanimity exists among Bible scholars as to who Gomer and Togarmah are, in general, the players in the Ezekiel War line up as the following:

Biblical Name	Modern Name
Rosh	--- Russia
Meshech	--- Moscow (Western capital of Russia)
Tubal	--- Tobulsk (Eastern capital of Russia)
Persia	--- Iran
Ethiopia	--- Ethiopia (possibly Sudan)
Libya	--- Libya
Gomer	--- Germany, or former Soviet Islamic states
Togarmah	--- Turkey
Gog	--- The evil spirit ruling Russia

The hordes of Gog, listed above will come against the tiny country of Israel to plunder and destroy it. What are the events that will precipitate this massive war? As stated in Chapter 2, I believe Syria will invade Israel. Israel will counterattack, leveling

Damascus. In the natural, it will be the Israeli destruction of Damascus that causes Russia and her allies to invade Israel. In the spiritual realm, it is God who ordains the attack.

Notice in the following verses depicting the Ezekiel War, where the Lord God Himself is speaking, commanding the nations to invade Israel:

> [7] *"Prepare yourself and be ready, you **and all your companies** that are gathered about you; and be a guard for them.*
>
> [8] *After many days you will be visited. In the latter years **you will come into the land** of those brought back from the sword and gathered from many people on the mountains of Israel, which had long been desolate; they were brought out of the nations, and now all of them dwell safely.*
>
> [9] ***You will ascend**, coming like a storm, covering the land like a cloud, **you and all your troops** and many peoples with you.*
>
> [10] ***Thus says the Lord God**: On that day it shall come to pass that thoughts will arise in your mind, and **you will make an evil plan**:*
>
> [11] *You will say, 'I will go up against a land of unwalled villages; I will go to a peaceful people who dwell safely, all of them dwelling without walls, and having neither bars nor gates'—*
>
> [12] *'to take plunder and to take booty, **to stretch out your hand** against the waste places that are again inhabited, and against a people gathered from the nations, who have acquired livestock and goods, who dwell in the midst of the land.'"*
>
> Ezekiel 38:7-12 (emphasis added)

God Ordains The Attack

The purpose of the war, from the adversary's point of view, is to take plunder and take booty, and to come against Israel, according to verse 12.

The nations of the world, including the United States, will lodge a diplomatic protest, but not interfere militarily:

> [13] *"Sheba, Dedan, the merchants of Tarshish, and **all their young lions will say to you,** 'Have you come to take plunder? Have you gathered your army to take booty, to carry away silver and gold, to take away livestock and goods, to take great plunder?'"*

Ezekiel 38:13 (emphasis added)

The Jews Will Win The War

Many Christian scholars consider Americans to be the "young lions of Tarshish." Tarshish is seen by various authors to be the northern Mediterranean area, Spain or England. Since the pilgrims were of European descent, any of the above definitions of Tarshish would qualify Americans to be their offspring, or young lions.

Against all odds, the Jews will win the war. To be more precise, the great God, Jehovah, will win the war. He has many weapons at His disposal. They include:

1) Earthquake: "Surely in that day there shall be a great earthquake in the land of Israel." Ezekiel 38:19
2) Military Might: "I will call for a sword against Gog in all My mountains..." Ezekiel 38:21
3) Friendly Fire: "...Every man's sword will be against his brother." Ezekiel 38:21
4) Pestilence and Bloodshed: "And I will bring him to judgment with pestilence and bloodshed..." Ezekiel 38:22
5) Rain, Hail, Fire and Brimstone: "I will rain down on him, on his troops, and on the many peoples who are with him, flooding rain, great hailstones, fire and brimstone." Ezekiel 38:22

It is my view that the war of Ezekiel 38 and 39 will precede the Tribulation Period. The Church will have her finest hour, as God uses us to bring in the great harvest for which we have prepared so long.

Thus, I will present the evidence, which I feel places the Ezekiel War before the Tribulation Period:

Event	Ezekiel War	Armageddon
Where it will be fought	Mountains of Israel Ezek. 38:21; 39:2	Valley of Armageddon Joel 3:14; Rev. 16:16
When it will be fought	6th Day, 'Latter Days' Ezek. 38:8; 16	7th Day, 'Day of the Lord' Zech. 14:1; Joel2:1; Obad. verse 15; Rev. 1:10
Concluded by	Treaty of Dan. 9:27	Jesus defeating the Nations - Zech. 14:3; Rev. 19:11-21
Nations participating	Russia, Iran, Ethiopia Libya, Germany, Turkey Ezek. 38:3, 5, 6	All Nations Zech 12:3; Zech. 14:2 Obad. verse 15
Position of Jerusalem when war begins	At peace Ezek. 38:11	'Trampled Down' Luke 21:24; Daniel 9:6
Position of Israelis when war begins	At peace Ezek. 38:14	Hiding in Petra Rev. 12:13-16; Isa. 16:4; Dan. 11:41
Purpose of the war	Bring in the harvest Ezek. 38:16, 23 Ezek. 39:7, 21	Set up the millennial reign with Israel presiding - Isa. 42:4; Zech. 14:16-21 Rev. 20:4

As I have indicated above, the Lord God Himself orders the invasion and then destroys the invaders. God, who is love, ordered the invasion. But, we might ask, why would He do that?

1) God is just, and must bring judgment on those who come against His chosen people.

   [19] *"For in My jealousy and in the fire of My wrath I have spoken…"*

                                                Ezekiel 38:19

2) God is merciful and this war will trigger the great world harvest.

[16] "...so that the nations may know Me, when I am hallowed in you, O Gog, before their eyes."
Ezekiel 38:16 (emphasis added)

[23] "Thus I will magnify Myself and sanctify Myself, and I will be known in the eyes of many nations. Then they shall know that I am the Lord."
Ezekiel 38:23 (emphasis added)

[7] "So I will make My holy name known in the midst of My people Israel, and I will not let them profane my name anymore. Then the nations shall know that I am the Lord, the Holy One in Israel."
Ezekiel 39:7 (emphasis added)

[21] "I will set My glory among the nations; all the nations shall see My judgment which I have executed, and My hand which I have laid on them."
Ezekiel 39:21 (emphasis added)

3) Israel will finally, as a nation, turn back to Jehovah, (however, they will not recognize their Messiah yet).

[22] "So the house of Israel shall know that I am the Lord their God from that day forward."
Ezekiel 39:22 (emphasis added)

Let us pause here to reflect on the lifestyle of the modern man and woman. Most of us watch television for two to four hours a day. Since the Vietnam conflict, we have become accustomed to watching war on television.

In the Iraqi War in 2003, we even had reporters "embedded" with the troops, so we could watch the war unfold, "play by play." How many hours a day did we watch television during the war? Thus it has become a part of our national psyche to see war "live and in color" on our television set.

Use your own imagination and project yourself into the days of the Ezekiel War. We are alarmed to see Russian troops moving into position! An alliance, much like our coalition against Iraq, will probably coalesce. Nations will decide to "teach Israel a lesson," once and for all. It has to happen, because God spoke it through Ezekiel.

A Muslim/Russian Alliance Formed To Teach Israel A Lesson

Television newsmen will be brining us updates, minute by minute. Christians will, no doubt, be holding prayer meetings around the clock: *"Father, let your will be done on earth as it is in heaven."* Nominal Christians and fence sitters will dust off the Word and check it out - Ezekiel 38 & 39.

Suddenly, the attack! Paratroopers descend on the mountains of Israel, *"covering the land like a cloud,"*—Ezekiel 38:9—*"all your troops and many peoples"* against a country of five million Jews. (Flashback to Gideon, who defeated innumerable Midianites with three hundred men.) Could it really be? Could the Bible be true?

And then, earthquake, sword, fire and brimstone, hail and rain. God reigns, He really is in control. Oh praise Him forever more!

Nations, yes nations, will come to the Lord. This will be the great harvest, for which we have waited so long. We will reap where we have not sown, the plowman will overtake the reaper, the former and the latter rain together. The knowledge of the glory of the Lord will cover the land as the water covers the seas, and we will be right in the middle of it all.

Christians open their Bibles to Ezekiel 38 and read fast and furious. Someone knocks at your door, the phone rings, the same question from every neighbor, every friend, "You're a Christian aren't you? What's happening?" Saints of God, learn it now, so you will be prepared. We must respond rightly. We will tell them, "This is only the beginning. God is judging the nations. Repent, and be saved. Accept Jesus and escape the wrath to come."

> [34] *"But take heed to yourselves, lest your hearts be weighed down with carousing, drunkenness, and cares of this life, and that Day come on you unexpectantly.*

³⁵For it will come as a snare on all those who dwell on the face of the whole earth.

*³⁶Watch therefore, and pray always **that you may be counted worthy to escape all these things that will come to pass**, and to stand before the Son of Man."*

Luke 21:34-36 (emphasis added)

*⁹**For God did not appoint us to wrath**, but to obtain salvation through our Lord Jesus Christ,*
¹⁰who died for us that whether we wake or sleep, we should live together with Him.

I Thessalonians 5:9-10 (emphasis added)

*¹⁰Because you have kept My command to persevere, I also will keep you from the hour of trial which shall **come upon the whole world, to test those who dwell on the earth.***
¹¹Behold, I am coming quickly! Hold fast what you have, that no one may take your crown.

Revelation 3:10-11 (emphasis added)

Dear saints of God, we are being called by the Holy Spirit in this hour to prepare. Now is the time to begin, if you have not already heard His command: longer seasons of prayer every day, taking communion, regular seasons of fasting, joining a cell group, studying and meditating in the Word, enrolling in that Bible Study offered by your Church, using your vacation to attend a good Christian seminar, etc. In short, it's time to set your heart on course, so you will be found *"without spot or wrinkle."*

Some will not accept the mantle, however. Sadly, they will miss the rapture. It will be their lot to see a Syrian diplomat travel to Israel, to negotiate a peace treaty with the victorious and ebullient Israelis. It is my view that his offer will include allowing the Jews to rebuild the temple on Mount Moriah. They have been yearning for a temple since 70 A.D., and it's too good a deal to turn

> **It's time to set your heart on course.**

down. Why will a Syrian be the negotiator? It may be that Syria will be the presiding nation at the United Nations Security Council, (they presently are presiding, as I write this book). Another possible reason is because the war was precipitated by the Syrian invasion of Israel. In any event, the Bible is clear, he is the antichrist, coming to the Israelis with a seven-year peace treaty:

> *27 "Then he shall confirm a covenant with many for one week; but in the middle of the week he shall bring an end to sacrifice and offering. And, on the wing of abominations shall be one who makes desolate, even until the consummation, which is determined, is poured out on the desolate."*
>
> Daniel 9:27

As we review Daniel 7:10 and 11 we notice that the first thing Daniel heard when the books were opened was the sound of the antichrist's voice.

> *10...The judgment was set, and the books were opened.*
> *11I beheld then because of the voice of the great words **which the horn spake**...*
>
> Daniel 7:10, 11 (KJV emphasis added)

Why was the antichrist's voice the first thing Daniel heard when Jesus opened the seals? The first four seals in Revelation Chapter 6 release the four horsemen of the Apocalypse. Does the first seal release the antichrist?

Read on to see if the Book of Revelation agrees with what we have just read here in the Book of Daniel.

CHAPTER 7

FTH

The Four Horsemen Explained

Part I - The Rider on the White Horse

3rd Chariot	On the White Horse	Repreesents Greece	The antichrist leaves Israel after the Peace Treaty of Dan. 9:27 and goes north to coalesce his base	Goes North	First to appear in Revelation

> [1]*Now I saw when the Lamb opened one of the seals; and I heard one of the four living creatures say with a voice like thunder, "Come and see."*
> [2]*And I looked, and behold, a white horse. He who sat on it had a bow; and a crown was given to him, and he went out conquering and to conquer.*
> Revelation 6:1-2

The earth is in chaos and confusion, due to the millions (and, perhaps, even billions) of saints who have disappeared in the rapture. Possibly the most powerful man on earth, the President of the United States, will be among the missing. America has been the conscience of the world. As peace-keeper, chastiser of rogue nations and provider of food, aid and medicine to the poor, she has had no equal. In the revival that accompanies the Ezekiel War, most Americans have recommitted their lives to the Lord Jesus. Therefore it is possible that two hundred million Americans depart in the rapture. (This is our fervent prayer.)

The world needs leadership. They turn for help to the brilliant diplomat who did what no one else could do - brought peace to the Middle East. This man, antichrist, is given a bow, military power, and a crown, legal authority, to assume power in the Arab World. Going north from Jerusalem, he unites the following Moslem nations, which are in chaos for the reasons listed:

Syria – devastated by the leveling of Damascus.
Iraq – still not stable after the Gulf War of 2003.
Iran and Turkey – These countries (as well as Russia, Libya and Ethiopia) have lost 84 percent of their young men in the Ezekiel War. Never, in modern warfare, has there been such devastation.

> [1]...*Behold, I am against thee, Oh Gog, the prince of Meshech and Tubal,*
> [2]***And I will turn thee back, and leave but a sixth part of thee,...***
> Ezekiel 39:1-2 KJV (emphasis added)

Lebanon – under the influence of Iran and Syria, they join the coalition for security reasons.

Therefore, we see the antichrist, an Islamic military leader, going north from Israel to create an alliance of these countries: Lebanon, Syria, Iran, Iraq and Turkey. In ancient times these countries had often been one big confederation known as the "Fertile Crescent." All pagan religions found their genesis in the Fertile Crescent where many deities were worshipped. Abraham was called out of the Fertile Crescent, to separate himself unto God.

I believe that the antichrist will rule out of the Fertile Crescent for the first three and a half years of the Tribulation Period. He will probably spend much time at the headquarters of the European Union, which is presently in Brussels, Belgium.

He will also have a "home base" out of which to operate. In ancient times, the leading cities of the Fertile Crescent were Ninevah and Babylon. Babylon will be the center of economic power during the Tribulation Period according to Zechariah 5:5-11 and Revelation Chapter 18. It is worthy to note that kings of Assyria, Babylon, Persia and Greece all had palaces in the ancient city of Babylon.

Alexander the Great, who conquered the known world, died in Babylon. The Bible clearly relates the antichrist to these four countries. He is referred to in Scripture as:

The Assyrian – Micah 5:5-6
The King of Babylon – Isaiah 14:4
He has feet like a bear (Persian implied) – Revelation 13:2
Son of Greece – Zechariah 9:13

I therefore conclude that the rider on the white horse, the antichrist, conquers the Arab world first, and sets up his headquarters in Babylon.

Part II - The Rider on the Red Horse

Before we embark on an explanation of the rider on the red horse, it is important to understand the history of monotheistic religion. Monotheistic religion is the belief in only one God. There are only three monotheistic religions: Judaism, Christianity, and Islam. All three of these religions hold Abraham to be their father. All three of these religions believe a ruler will rise up from their religion at the end of days to rule the world. Amazingly, all three are correct, setting up the climax of human history!

Jewish doctrine states:

I believe, with complete faith that Messiah will come.

Christianity doctrine states:

God will send Jesus, whom heaven must receive until the time of the restoration of all things (Acts 3:21).

Moslem doctrine states:

Fight until all declare there is no God but Allah, and Mohammad is his prophet.

Furthermore, the Moslems are waiting for an Islamic prophet to come out of the desert at the end of days to lead the entire world into the Islamic faith (see Page 43).

Islam leaves no room for compromise. It is their avowed purpose to win the world. A recent Al Qaida memorandum, run on an Islamic web site, adjures Moslems to **"...return to the path, to**

separate themselves from nonbelievers, to become their enemies and to fight holy war against them by money, word, and weapons. This enemy must be fought, there is no other way but to…eradicate it."[12]

It is my opinion that Jews, Christians, and Moslems will all see their heroes on the center stage of world history very soon. First, the antichrist will appear as the rider on the white horse. He will be a Moslem military leader. Seven years later, the Jews will see Messiah, as He sets His feet on the Mount of Olives. No surprise to those who accepted Jesus after the rapture, the Jewish Messiah is none other than our own Lord and Savior, Jesus Christ.

Let us now consider the rider on the red horse.

1st Chariot	On the Red Horse	Represents Babylon (Iraq)	Take a sword (Islam) throughout the earth	Goes to the whole earth	Second to appear in Revelation

> [3]*When He opened the second seal, I heard the second living creature saying, "Come and see."*
> [4]*Another horse, fiery red, went out. And it was granted to the one who sat on it to take peace from the earth, and that people should kill one another; and there was given to him a great sword.*
>
> Revelation 6:3-4

It is interesting to note that the rider on the red horse is the only horseman given permission to go throughout the whole earth. Approximately 1.5 billion of the 6 billion people living today are Moslem. Mosques are springing up in traditionally Christian countries at an alarmingly rapid rate.

Martyrdom of infidels – those who do not accept Allah, and Mohammad as his prophet – has historically been an acceptable way to spread Islam. Thus, we are not surprised to see that the rider on the red horse is given a "great sword." I believe the "great sword" represents Islam and the Moslem fundamentalists who spread their faith by the sword. Decapitation has long been a method of execution in Eastern cultures. The Philistines beheaded King Saul (I Samuel 31:9) and Herod had John the Baptist beheaded

(Matthew 14:8). In recent history, Daniel Pearl, a Jewish New York Times reporter, was beheaded by the Pakistanis in 2002. Since 2002, dozens of people have been beheaded by Islamic extremists. Therefore, we should not be surprised to learn that martyrdom by decapitation will be used against followers of Jesus during the Tribulation Period:

> *⁴And I saw thrones, and they sat on them, and judgment was committed to them. I saw the **souls of those who had been beheaded** for their witness to Jesus and for the word of God, who had not worshiped the beast or his image, and had not received his mark on their foreheads or on their hands. And they lived and reigned with Christ for a thousand years.*
>
> Revelation 20:4 (emphasis added)

The world had expected the antichrist to usher in an era of peace and security. He was the architect of the brilliant peace plan after the Ezekiel War (see Page 67). Instead, he gives his Islamic followers permission to go throughout the world, spreading the Moslem ideology by the sword. Therefore, there will be no peace. The great apostle Paul had forewarned them:

> *²For you yourselves know perfectly that the day of the Lord so comes as a thief in the night.*
> *³For when they say, **"Peace and safety!"** then **sudden destruction comes upon them**, as labor pains upon a pregnant woman. And they shall not escape.*
>
> I Thessalonians 5:2-3 (emphasis added)

The rider on the white horse, the antichrist, goes north. The rider on the red horse goes to the whole world. Next, we will consider the rider on the black horse, who also travels north.

Part III - The rider on the Black Horse

3rd Chariot	On the White Horse	Repreesents Greece	The antichrist leaves Israel after the Peace Treaty of Dan. 9:27 and goes north to coalesce his base	Goes North	First to appear in Revelation

We see in Zechariah 6:6 that the rider on the black horse actually **precedes** the antichrist (the rider on the white horse) into the north country.

> *⁶The one with the black horses is going to the north country, the white are going after them, and the dappled are going toward the south country.*
>
> Zechariah 6:6

In other words, famine and devastation are already causing severe problems in Iran before Jesus opens the seals. The Ancient Medo-Persian Empire included Iran, Iraq, Turkey and Southern Russia.

The devastation had already begun during the Ezekiel War (see chart on page 30). Iran and the other combatants had suffered a casualty rate of a staggering 84 percent of their troops in that war.

> *¹Therefore, thou son of man, prophesy against Gog, and say, Thus saith the Lord God; Behold, I am against thee, O Gog, the chief prince of Meshech and Tubal:*
> *²And I will turn thee back, and leave but **the sixth part of thee**, and will cause thee to come up from the north parts, and will bring thee upon the mountains of Israel:*
>
> Ezekiel 39:1-2 (KJV emphasis added)

Such high casualty rates had occurred in Old Testament times. (Numbers 31:7; Joshua 6:21; I Kings 11:15 - 16; II Kings 19:35)

But never, in a modern military confrontation, had a nation lost 5/6 of its soldiers. God seems to have punished not only the military, but also the homelands of these armies (Ezekiel 38:2 indicates that "Magog" refers to Russia).

> *⁶And I will send fire on Magog and on those who live in security in the coastlands. Then they shall know that I am the Lord.*
>
> Ezekiel 39:6

Let us consider the rider on the black horse according to the translation of Zechariah 6:8 provided for us by David Baron (see page 48).

```
See those who go to the north country
have caused my anger to rest on the
north country.
```

In the spirit realm, the Ezekiel War had been precipitated by the bonding together of two very powerful and very evil spirits: Islam and Communism. God's anger had rested on the countries whose leaders embraced these spirits. Thus, these countries had reaped judgment: Iran, Syria, Turkey, Russia and possibly Germany. All of the above, the north country, have been bastions of anti-Semitism for generations. They have persecuted God's chosen people, the apple of His eye. Beginning during the Ezekiel War, and progressing through the Tribulation Period, they will be reaping all the evil they have sown.

John sees that the rider on the black horse, who was sent to the north country, has a pair of scales in his hand. The only direct quotation John hears, during the

The bonding together of... Islam and Communism

episode with the four horsemen, is spoken when the black horse is released. John hears a voice speaking from heaven. Let us consider what the voice says:

> *⁶And I heard a voice in the midst of the four living creatures saying, "A quart of wheat for a denarius; and three quarts of barley for a denarius: and do not harm the oil and the wine."*
>
> Revelation 6:6

In John's day a denarius was one day's wages for a laborer. This quote seems to imply that an entire day's pay will be needed to buy mere staple foods to subsist on. In fact, this kind of severe poverty already exists in some third world countries.

Some Biblical scholars believe the words *"and do not harm the oil and wine"* indicate that a few, probably the leadership of these countries, will live in excessive luxury while their people suffer. We saw a clear picture of that scenario in Saddam Hussein's Iraq.

Thus, we have a dismal scene in the countries north of Israel. Scarcity of food, starvation which causes disease to flourish, inconsolable grief at the loss of so much life, and a shortage of manpower due to the deaths of the military. Conditions are ripe for this Hitler-like antihero, who rides to the north country. The people will no doubt be eager to hear his diabolical plan to make them powerful and wealthy again!

Part IV - The Rider on the Green Horse

4th Chariot	On the Dappled\Green	Represents Rome	Given power over 1/4 of the earth. The evil twins, "Death and Hell," kill with war, hunger, beasts of the earth and their own evil spiritual power.	Goes South	Fourth to appear in Revelation

Before we discuss the riders associated with the fourth and final horse, we must clarify who they are. Their names are Death and Hell, and they appear together throughout the Bible.

To understand Death and Hell, we must first comprehend this truth:

In the Bible the same name is often given to people and to a geographic location.

Thus, we will see that Death and Hell are evil spirits, and also a place where spirits go.

We will look at several examples, to help solidify this concept in our thinking, in the chart below.

NAME	REPRESENTS PEOPLE/SPIRITS	REPRESENTS GEOGRAPHICAL LOCATION
Jerusalem	Matt. 23:37 "O Jerusalem, Jerusalem...I wanted to gather your children together."	John 5:1 "Jesus went up to Jerusalem."
Israel	Matt. 2:6 "...Who will shepherd My people Israel?"	Matt. 2:20 "...go into the land of Israel."
Bride of Christ	Rev. 19:7 "...the marriagae of the Lamb has come and His wife has made herself ready."	Rev. 21:9, 10 "Come, I will show you the bride, the Lamb's wife..and (he) showed me the great city."
Death and Hell	Rev. 6:8 "...the name of him who sat on it was Death and Hades followed with him."	Rev. 20:13 "...Death and Hades delivered up the dead who were in them."

Death and Hell are seen throughout the Bible, working together. Their purpose is always to destroy men's souls. We presume that Death encourages human beings to continue in sin until it kills them (Romans 6:21, 23). Then Hell scoops them up at the moment of death and carries them off to hell. Let us consider some of the nefarious deeds of Death and Hell:

1) They incited the demented King Saul to try to destroy David.

   ⁶The sorrows of Sheol surround me; the snares of death confronted me.

   II Samuel 22:6

2) They persuaded the rulers of Jerusalem to look to Egypt instead of Jehovah for protection.

   ¹⁴Therefore hear the word of the Lord, you scornful

men, Who rule the people who are in Jerusalem.
*[15]Because you have said, "We have made a covenant
with death, And with Sheol we are in agreement."*

Isaiah 28:14, 15

3) The Babylonians covenanted with Death and Hell. Death
   and Hell assisted them in destroying Jerusalem in 586
   B.C.:

*[5]Because he enlarges his desire as hell, And he is
like death, and cannot be satisfied, He gathers to
himself all nations and heaps up for himself all
peoples.*

Habakkuk 2:5

4) The apostle Paul quotes the final victory over them in I
   Corinthians 15:55:

*[55]O Death, where is your sting? O Hades, where is
your victory?"*

5) Jesus Himself refers to them as a place:

*[18]"I am He who lives, and was dead, and behold, I
am alive forevermore, Amen., And I have the keys
of Hades and of Death.*

Revelation 1:18

As we read Revelation 6:8, we notice that only Death sits on the
green horse. Hell, or Hades, follows with him. We will now investigate
their assignment, as the judgment of planet earth continues.

*[7]When He opened the fourth seal, I heard the voice
of the fourth living creature saying, "Come and
see."
[8]So I looked, and behold, a pale (green) horse. And
the name of him who sat on it was Death, and
Hades followed with him. And power was given to
them over a fourth of the earth, to kill with sword,
with hunger, with death, and by the beasts of the
earth.*

Revelation 6:7, 8 (parenthesis added)

At the beginning of the Tribulation Period, the revived Roman Empire will probably approximate the borders of the European Union. The Europeans have a mindset foreign to independent-minded American thinking. They want to give up their national identity. They have been gradually assimilating into one group over fifty years for this goal — they want to be the most powerful political and economic bloc in the world!

The European Economic Community was founded in 1957 with a document called the "Treaty of Rome." It is my view that the desire to give up national identity to revive an ancient political entity is being driven by evil spirits. Could those evil spirits be Death and Hell?

According to Revelation 6:7 these spirits have the power to kill with the sword. We see this sword as military and political power. It is interesting to note that the United Nations transferred the task of policing Bosnia to the European Union on January 1, 2003.[13] Furthermore, in May of 2003, the European Union ordered "180 Airbus A400 military transport jumbo jets with the capacity to deploy up to 20,000 troops." [14] As I write this book, a mighty military machine is being assembled within the European Union.

How will Death and Hell, the spirits we believe are ruling the European Union, *"kill with hunger"* in Revelation 6:7? To understand this political maneuver, it is necessary to understand genetically engineered food.

Genetically engineered food, pioneered in the United States, is food that has been scientifically altered to resist disease and insects without excessive pesticides. Often, it is also engineered to be more

> **A mighty military machine is being assembled within the European Union!**

nutritious. Approximately sixty to seventy percent of America's exported grain is genetically engineered.[15]

As part of its radical, left wing environmental policy, the European Union objects to these foods. They are blocking the export of genetically engineered foods from the United States, through the United Nations, to third world countries. Thus we see that Death and Hell are already killing with hunger.

The prophet Daniel described the revived Roman Empire with two separate analogies (see pages 35, 55 and 57). As the feet of Nebuchadnezzar's image, it looked like this:

> *40And the fourth kingdom shall be as strong as iron, inasmuch as iron breaks in pieces and shatters everything; and like iron that crushes, that kingdom will break in pieces and crush all the others.*
>
> Daniel 2:40

As the fourth great beast in Daniel, Chapter 7, he saw it like this:

> *19Then I wished to know the truth about the fourth beast, which was different from all the others, exceedingly dreadful, with its **teeth of iron and its nails of bronze**, which devoured, broke in pieces, and trampled the residue with its feet;*
> *20and the ten horns that were on its head, and the other horn which came up, before which three fell, namely, that horn which had eyes and a mouth which spoke pompous words, whose appearance was greater than his fellows.*
>
> Daniel 7:19-20 (emphasis added)

Notice that in the image of the great beast its teeth are iron, representing Rome. It's nails are bronze, representing the Syrian Greek antichrist.

According to the Book of Revelation, the first direction the green horseman goes is south. Remember that the end time struggles are primarily a spiritual battle for wealth and power!

After the rapture, the earth will be in chaos, with billions of people raptured. America will be greatly weakened, since two thirds of her population went to heaven. (This is my fervent prayer.) The antichrist went north, as we have already seen. The Europeans, the dominant world power since the rapture, see antichrist's power rising.

To counter his fame, Rome turns south to woo Egypt and the rest of Africa. They'd better grab what power they can, to maintain their primacy! Egypt, Libya and Ethiopia ally themselves with Rome, completing the Revival of the ancient Roman Empire. (It is my view that the three kings the antichrist attacks and defeats mid tribulation are three of Rome's Islamic allies: Egypt, Libya and Ethiopia. Let the readers study Daniel 11:40, 42, 43 in many translations to understand this concept.)

I conclude this chapter with the release of the four horsemen, the beginning of the seven year era known as the Tribulation Period. The reader is encouraged to continue on, reading what John, the beloved apostle, was so diligent to record.

We began this chapter with the earth in chaos, due to the rapture of the Church. Dear reader, are you ready for the rapture? Some will answer like this: "I don't want to be raptured. I like my life the way it is." But life is not going to continue on in the way it is.

Once women were told they could have an abortion in the first trimester, when there was only "a mass of protoplasm" in their uterus. Today, full term babies' brains are sucked out in the birth canal while they are being delivered.

Once terrorism occurred in strange lands far away among uncivilized people. Today, no one is safe anywhere, not even in America.

Once, a bank robbery made headlines in the local newspapers. Today CEO's of high tech companies bilk their shareholders out of billions of dollars.

Once, prostitution was called a "victimless crime." Today, human trafficking, selling children as sex slaves, goes on in all countries, even America.

Once, what people did in their own bedrooms, behind closed doors, was their own business. Today, those same people, have lewd parades in our major cities, handcuffing and whipping each other as they march along.

Jesus promised that at the end of the age, evil would become so evil that everyone would be able to recognize it.

[24]Another parable He put forth to them, saying:
"The kingdom of heaven is like a man who sowed
good seed in his field;
[25]but while men slept, his enemy came and sowed
tares among the wheat and went his way.
[26]But when the grain had sprouted and produced a
crop, then the tares also appeared."

[30]Let both grow together until the harvest, and **at**
the time of harvest I will say to the reapers, "First
gather together the tares and bind them in
bundles to burn them, but gather the wheat into
my barn."

[39]The enemy who sowed them is the devil, **the**
harvest is the end of the age, *and the reapers are*
the angels.

Matthew 13:24-26, 30, 39 (emphasis added)

We are now in harvest time, the end of the age. The tares are being bundled, which is why sin is now so frank and bold. **You will not be able to continue in your comfortable life, but you can be part of the glorious Church.**

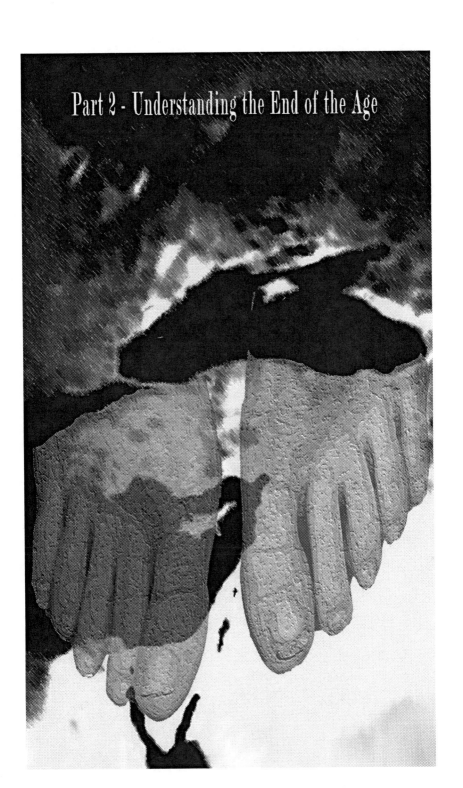

Part 2 - Understanding the End of the Age

CHAPTER 8
FTH

The Glorious Future
of the Glorious Church

God sees three groups of people on the earth: the Jews, the nations, and the Church.

> *32Give none offence, neither to the Jews, nor to the Gentiles, nor to the church of God:*
>
> 1 Corinthians 10:32 (KJV)

Much confusion has entered into our understanding of the Church's role by trying to fit the Church into Old Testament Scriptures. Truly there are layers of meaning in Scriptures, and we may appropriate them for our walk of faith. However, the Old Testament was written primarily to the Jews and nations. The role of the Jews will be considered in greater detail in Chapter 12. To understand the destiny of the nations, let us consider the words of Jesus Himself. He refers in this passage to events after His return to earth at Armageddon, to save the Jews from annihilation:

> *31When the Son of Man comes in His glory, and all the holy angels with Him, then He will sit on the throne of His glory.*
> *32All the nations will be gathered before Him, and He will separate them one from another, as a shepherd divides his sheep from the goats.*
> *33And He will set the sheep on His right hand, but the goats on the left.*
> *34Then the King will say to those on His right hand,*

> *"Come, you blessed of My Father, inherit the*
> *kingdom prepared for you from the foundation of*
> *the world:"*
>
> *[41]Then He will also say to those on the left hand,*
> *"Depart from Me, you cursed, into the everlasting*
> *fire prepared for the devil and his angels:"*
>
> Matthew 25: 31–34, 41

Thus, Jesus will allow the sheep nations to live on earth during the Millennium. The goat nations will go to hell. The stage is being set for Jesus' return, even as I write this book. Nations are polarizing, for good or for evil. The litmus test, so to speak, is this: Do you love God and His chosen people, the Jews?

Those who will be judged "sheep" nations will love and protect the Jews. The "goat" nations will hate and abuse them.

Both King David and his worship leader Asaph were given glimpses of the end of this age. They must have had very dramatic conversations, as they compared notes on what God had revealed to them!

WHAT KING DAVID WROTE:

> *[1]Why do the nations rage, And the people plot a vain*
> *thing?*
> *[2]The kings of the earth set themselves, And the rulers*
> *take counsel together, Against the Lord and against*
> *His Anointed, saying,*
> *[3]"Let us break Their bonds in pieces And cast away*
> *Their cords from us."*
>
> Psalm 2:1–3

Today as the kings of the earth (United Nations, Arab Confederation and European Union) set themselves against God and Israel, they are inviting the judgments of God to fall on them.

WHAT ASAPH WROTE:

> *[1]Do not keep silent, O God! Do not hold Your peace,*
> *And do not be still, O God!*
> *[2]For behold, Your enemies make a tumult; And those*

who hate You have lifted up their head.
³They have taken crafty counsel against Your people,
And consulted together against Your sheltered
ones.
⁴They have said, **"Come, and let us cut them off**
from being a nation, That the name of Israel may
be remembered no more."

Psalm 83:1–4 (emphasis added)

It is the ultimate end of those who would try to cut off Israel from being a nation to be severely disciplined by Jesus Himself.

Dear reader, if you commit your life to Jesus, you can escape the wrath to come. By accepting Jesus, you can extricate yourself from the group called "the nations," and become a part of the group called "the Church." Jesus' own Word declares the end for those who reject Him: *"...the furnace of fire. There will be wailing and gnashing of teeth"* (Matthew 13:42).

The world's answer rings out loudly, "I don't want to serve any God who sends people to hell." Neither do I. **God does not send people to hell!** People choose hell. God is a Spirit; He made man in His image. As God can have no end, neither can we. You must live on in perpetuity, because spirits can never cease to be.

The Father dwells in a wonderful planet called heaven, with His son Jesus sitting at His right hand. Everyone there has a home (John 14:2), an assignment, and a "life." Much time in heaven is spent in worship services, praising the Father and Jesus. Would you enjoy doing that?

If your answer is a resounding "No, Never!" then friend, you just chose hell. You see there are only two places for spirits to go when they leave the body.

Hell wasn't created for you; it was created for the devil and his angels (Matthew 25:41). However, it had to be enlarged to accommodate rebellious people (Isaiah 5:14). Ultimately, you must choose for yourself. You will not be able to stand before God and "Lord, I didn't know." By virtue of the fact that you are reading

> **God does not send people to hell. People *choose* hell!**

this book, and by the many other witnesses God has sent into your life—you know! All you will be able to say is, "Lord, I chose not to believe." Dear friend, I earnestly adjure you, do not select that path.

> *[9]...I have set before you life and death, blessing and cursing; **therefore choose life**, that both you and your descendants may live;*
>
> *[20]**that you may love the Lord your God,** that you may obey His voice, and that you may cling to Him, for He is your life and the length of your days;..."*
>
> Deuteronomy 30:19-20 (emphasis added)

And now, dear reader, prepare to look into the future of the glorious Church. There are three possible roads for you to travel while you still live on planet earth. You may belong to only one group: the Jews, the nations, or the Church. (1 Corinthians 10:32)

If you choose to be part of the Church, here is your destiny:

1. Walk into greater joy and power as you grow in love and learn to appropriate what Jesus died to give you (see page 173 of this book)
2. Be raptured before the Tribulation begins
3. Enjoy the seven year celebration in heaven, while the earth is being judged
4. Rule and reign over the entire universe with Jesus forever (Matthew 24:47; Revelation 21:7)

[Editor's Note: Part 3 of From The Hidden, entitled "It Really Is Happily Ever After" will be published soon. It will explain in greater detail the eternal destiny of the glorious Church.]

THE RAPTURE OF THE CHURCH

Jesus spoke of the catching away of the Church several times.

> *[40] And this is the will of Him who sent Me, that everyone who sees the Son and believes in Him may have everlasting life; and **I will raise him up***

at the last day.

John 6:40 (emphasis added)

He adjures us to pray, that we might escape the Tribulation.

> [36]*Watch therefore, and pray always **that you may be counted worthy to escape** all these things that will come to pass, **and to stand before the Son of Man**.*
>
> Luke 21:36 (emphasis added)

Sometimes the disciples did not "catch on" to all that Jesus taught them. For example, Jesus clearly directed them to take the gospel to the whole world.

> [15]*And He said to them, "Go into all the world and preach the gospel to every creature."*
>
> Mark 16:15

However, it wasn't until Peter saw the sheet with the unclean animals and went to Cornelius' house in Acts 10:45 that they comprehended this truth.

Likewise, while Jesus had taught on the "catching away" of the Church before the Tribulation, the disciples didn't seem to understand (the popular name for the catching away is the rapture of the Church).

God allowed the great apostle Paul to clearly relate the doctrine of the rapture of the Church. A timeline of some of the events in Paul's life related to his rapture teaching can be found in the chart below.

Jesus Crucified	Paul Saved On The Road To Damascus	Paul Wrote 1 & 2 Thessalonians	Paul Wrote 1 Corinthians	Paul Martyred In Rome
32 A.D.	35 A.D.	50 A.D.	56 A.D.	66-67 A.D.

The books of Thessalonians were the first epistles ever written. That makes the rapture doctrine one of Christianity's oldest beliefs!

1. Paul saw Jesus in visions (Acts 22:18; Acts 26:12-18).
2. Paul visited heaven (2 Corinthians 12:2).
3. Paul learned about Communion directly from Jesus (1 Corinthians 11:23).

We will now study exactly what Paul revealed to the infant Church in the first letter he ever wrote in 50 A.D., regarding the rapture of the Church.

> *[14]For if we believe that Jesus died and rose again, even so God will bring with Him* **those who sleep in Jesus**.
>
> *[15]For this we say to you by the word of the Lord, that we who are alive and remain until the coming of the Lord* **will by no means precede those who are asleep**.
>
> *[16]For the Lord Himself will descend from heaven with a shout, with the voice of an archangel, and with the trumpet of God. And the dead in Christ will rise first.*
>
> **[17]Then we who are alive and remain shall be caught up together with them in the clouds to meet the Lord in the air.** *And thus we shall always be with the Lord.*
>
> 1 Thessalonians 4:14-17 (emphasis added)

(Paul uses the word "sleep" instead of the offensive word "dead" much as we use the term "passed away" today.)

In the next chapter he warns them that the Day of the Lord (The Great Tribulation) will come as a surprise to the nations.

> *[1]But concerning the times and the seasons, brethren, you have no need that I should write to you.*
>
> *[2]For you yourselves know perfectly that the day of the Lord so comes as a thief in the night.*
>
> *[3]For when they say, "Peace and safety!" then sudden destruction comes upon them, as labor pains upon a pregnant woman. And they shall not escape.*

> *⁴But you, brethren, are not in darkness, so that this*
> *Day should not overtake you as a thief.*
>
> ***⁹For God did not appoint us to wrath, but to obtain***
> ***salvation through our Lord Jesus Christ,***
> ***¹⁰who died for us, that whether we wake or sleep,***
> ***we should live together with Him.***
>
> 1 Thessalonians 5:1-4; 9-10 (emphasis added)

In the Scripture above, we have an example of the Sower (God the Father) sowing the seed (the doctrine of the rapture). According to Mark 4:15, *"...Satan comes immediately and takes away the word that was sown in their hearts."* That is exactly what happened in Thessalonica! Satan immediately sent false teachers to the Thessalonian Church to steal this doctrine of the rapture. As soon as he could, also in 50 A.D., Paul wrote 2 Thessalonians to set the Church back on track. He rebuts a lying doctrine, introduced *"by spirit* (false implied) *or by word or by letter,"* that the Day of the Lord had already come.

> *¹Now, brethren, concerning the coming of our Lord*
> *Jesus Christ and our gathering together to Him,*
> *we ask you,*
> *²not to be soon shaken in mind or troubled, either*
> *by spirit or by word or by letter, as if from us, as*
> *though the day of Christ had come.*
> *³Let no one deceive you by any means; **for that Day***
> ***will not come unless the falling away comes first,***
> ***and the man of sin is revealed, the son of***
> ***perdition,***
> *⁴who opposes and exalts himself above all that is*
> *called God or that is worshiped, so that he sits as*
> *God in the temple of God, showing himself that he*
> *is God.*
>
> 2 Thessalonians 2:1-4 (emphasis added)

After Paul corrected the Church in the second letter, the rapture became "settled doctrine" and prevailed as truth until the 4th century

A.D. At that time, various false doctrines began to emerge that are still prevalent in the Church today.

Paul discussed the rapture doctrine again in 56 A.D. In 1 Corinthians 15 he expounds in a scholarly way on the general topic of resurrection. First, he waxes eloquent on the subject of Our Risen Lord. He then discusses the resurrection of the dead saints, building toward the end of the age to a great and thrilling mystery!

> **[51] Behold, I tell you a mystery: We shall not all sleep, but we shall all be changed—**
>
> [52] *in a moment, in the twinkling of an eye, at the last trumpet. For the trumpet will sound, and **the dead will be raised incorruptible, and we shall be changed.***
>
> [53] *For this corruptible must put on incorruption, and this mortal must put on immortality.*
>
> [54] *So when this corruptible has put on incorruption, and this mortal has put on immortality,*
> *then shall be brought to pass the saying that is written: "Death is swallowed up in victory."*
>
> 1 Corinthians 15:51-54 (emphasis added)

(Again, Paul uses the word "sleep" instead of the offensive word "die" just as we use the term "passed away" today.)

To further solidify the concept of the rapture in our thinking, we will contrast New Testament teaching with the writings of Isaiah. Scholars refer to Chapters 24 through 27 of Isaiah as the "Little Apocalypse." We are not surprised to find the

...not surprised to find the doctrine of the rapture in the Old Testament.

doctrine of the rapture in the Old Testament; saints of the Old Testament will join us at the rapture.

DOCTRINAL TRUTH	BOOK OF ISAIAH	NEW TESTAMENT
The righteous dead shall live	*Your dead shall live (*Old Testament saints); together with my dead body (*of Christ) they shall arise.* Isaiah 26:19	The dead in Christ will rise first. 1 Thessalonians 4:16 *The dead will be raised incorruptible…* 1 Corinthians 15:52
God says "come" to believers still alive	*Come, my people* Isaiah 26:20	Come up here Revelation 4:1 Revelation 11:12
There is an open door in heaven.	*And shut your doors behind you* Isaiah 26: 20**	After these things I looked, and behold, a door standing open Revelation 4:1
God protects the righteous from wrath	*Hide yourself, as it were, for a little moment, until the indignation is past.* Isaiah 26:20	Watch therefore, and pray always that you may be counted worthy to escape all these things that will come to pass, and to stand before the Son of Man. Luke 21:36

*AUTHOR'S OPINION

****Another passage that refers to the door being shut after the rapture can be found in Matthew 25:10 (see page 97)**

THE MARRIAGE SUPPER OF THE LAMB

When Jesus lived on earth, it was a Jewish custom for the bride to come, after the marriage, and live in her father-in-law's home. Before the wedding, the groom was required to add on to the father's house a suitable dwelling place. Jesus is presently fulfilling the role of our Bridegroom.

> *[2]"In My Father's house are many mansions; if it were not so, I would have told you. **I go to prepare***

a place for you.
*³And if I go and prepare a place for you, **I will come
again and receive you to Myself;** that where I am
there you may be also."*

John 14:2-3 (emphasis added)

The Apostle Paul explained further that we are united with Jesus
in a spiritual union, or marriage.

*²⁴Therefore, just as the church is subject to
Christ,..."*

*²⁷that He might present her to Himself a glorious
church, not having spot or wrinkle or any such
thing, but that she should be holy and without
blemish.*

*³⁰For we are members of His body, of His flesh and
of His bones.*
*³¹For this reason a man shall leave his father and
mother and be joined to his wife, **and the two shall
become one flesh.***
*³²**This is a great mystery, but I speak concerning
Christ and the church.***

Ephesians 5:24, 27, 30–32 (emphasis added)

In the following passage the Bible clearly states we will receive
our reward in heaven, while the nations are being judged on earth
(see also 2 Timothy 4:8).

*¹⁷saying: "We give You thanks, O Lord God
Almighty, The One who is and who was and who
is to come, Because You have taken Your great
power and reigned.*
*¹⁸The nations were angry, and Your wrath has come,
And the time of the dead, that they should be
judged, **And that You should reward Your servants
the prophets and the saints, And those who fear***

> ***Your name,*** *small and great, ... "*
> Revelation 11:17-18 (emphasis added)

Notice this chilling fact. In the following parable of the Wedding Feast, Jesus seems to imply that only fifty percent of professing Christians will be raptured.

> *¹Then the kingdom of heaven shall be likened to ten virgins who took their lamps and went out to meet the bridegroom.*
> *²**Now five of them were wise, and five were foolish.***
> *³Those who were **foolish took** their lamps and took **no oil with them.***
> *⁴but **the wise took oil** in their vessels with their lamps.*
> *⁵But while the bridegroom was delayed, they all slumbered and slept.*
> *⁶And at midnight a cry was heard: "Behold, the bridegroom is coming; go out to meet him!"*
> *⁷Then all those virgins arose and trimmed their lamps.*
> *⁸And the foolish said to the wise, "Give us some of your oil, for our lamps are going out."*
> *⁹But the wise answered, saying, "No, lest there should not be enough for us and you; but go rather to those who sell, and buy for yourselves."*
> *¹⁰And while they went to buy, the bridegroom came, and **those who were ready went in with him to the wedding; and the door was shut.***
> *¹¹**Afterward the other virgins came also,** saying, "Lord, Lord, open to us!"*
> *¹²But He answered and said, **"Assuredly, I say to you, I do not know you."***
> Matthew 25:1–12 (emphasis added)

Only three verses before the rapture, which occurs in Revelation 4:1, Jesus gives one final invitation to the marriage supper of the Lamb.

> *[20]Behold, I stand at the door and knock. If anyone hears My voice and opens the door, I will come in to him **and dine with him, and he with Me**.*
>   Revelation 3:20 (emphasis added)

Those who profess to be Christians, but aren't, are listed in the Book of Revelation. They include the following groups of "professing Christians," who Jesus says need to repent:

1. They have lost their love for Jesus (Revelation 2:4).
2. They tolerate immorality, idolatry and/or heresy (Revelation 2:14, 20).
3. They are (spiritually) dead (Revelation 3:2).
4. They are lukewarm and put their trust in their money (Revelation 3:15, 17).
5. They embrace replacement theology. They say they are "Zion" in their theology. Jesus says they are of the "synagogue of satan" (Revelation 3:9).

After the rapture, those Christians who missed the rapture will split into two groups.

1. Those who recognize they were in sin. They will repent and be the "underground Church" of the Tribulation. They will link up with the Jews to win the lost. They will suffer greatly and many will be martyred (Revelation 6:9-11; 20:4).
2. Those who refuse to recognize their sin. They will be the apostate Church prophesied by Paul (2 Timothy 4:3-4). The apostate Church is discussed in detail in Chapter 11.

> **Notice this chilling fact...**
> **Jesus seems to imply that only 50% of professing Christians will be raptured!**

To continue on with the Bridegroom paradigm, notice that Jesus identified Himself as our Bridegroom very early in His ministry.

> *[19]And Jesus said to them, "Can the friends of the bridegroom fast while the bridegroom is with them? As long as they have the bridegroom with*

them they cannot fast.

*20But the days will come when the bridegroom will
be taken away from them, and then they will fast
in those days."*

Mark 2:19, 20

As I write this book, the call by Jesus to the Church to "Come up here" is only a few short years away. Revelation knowledge of this holy event is pouring out on the Church, by the Holy Spirit, all over the globe. Our spirits soar as this exciting time draws near...

*7Let us be glad and rejoice and give Him glory, for
the marriage of the Lamb has come, and **His wife
has made herself ready.***

*8And to her it was granted to be arrayed in fine
linen, clean and bright, for the fine linen is the
righteous acts of the saints.*

*9Then he said to me, "Write: **'Blessed are those
who are called to the marriage supper of the
Lamb!'"** And he said to me, "These are the true
sayings of God."*

Revelation 19:7–9 (emphasis added)

Saints of God, it is my contention that we are that generation who will hear the words "come up here." We are the generation that death cannot destroy! The Church has a glorious future, and we are fulfilling it in this hour. Here is our mandate:

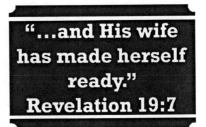

"...and His wife has made herself ready."
Revelation 19:7

1. To be holy, without spot or wrinkle.
2 To lead millions, even billions of people to the Lord Jesus.
3 To depart in victory, and meet the Lord in the air.
4. From then on, and forever, to be with God!

CHAPTER

9

FTH

Ten Kings that Rule the World

The belief that this present age would conclude with ten kings ruling the earth has been accepted by Bible scholars since antiquity. Daniel first alluded to the ten kings in the book of Daniel, written about 600 BC. They are the ten toes in Nebuchadnezzar's image in Daniel Chapter 2. Seven hundred years later, John expounded on them in Revelation. They are pictured here as the ten horns (Revelation 12:3; 13:1). Let us unveil eight of the ten kings, which Scripture clearly identifies. Before we begin, it is important to understand that to Jehovah, Israel is the center of the earth (Ezekiel 5:5) All of human history revolves around this Holy Land. In the end, whoever wins Jerusalem will rule the world.

Therefore, to understand who the kings are, we must answer this question:

Who are the seven kingdoms that have oppressed Israel throughout history?

Below is a key to help you memorize the answer.

Key – 7 Gentile Kingdoms

Every Ancient Biblical Message-Promise God Reveals Rightly

(Memorize the phrase and use this key to remember
the name of the seven kingdoms.)

Egypt, Assyria, Babylon, Medo-Persia, Greece, Rome, Revived Rome

---

(You will learn more from this book if you commit the key to memory.)

Notice in the following Scriptures that the ten horns (kings) **come out of the seven heads** (kingdoms that oppressed Israel).

Satan is ... *a great fiery red dragon **having seven heads and ten horns,** and **seven diadems** on his heads* Revelation 12:3 (emphasis added).

Antichrist is ...*a beast rising up out of the sea, **having seven heads and ten horns,** and on his horns **ten crowns**...* Revelation 13:1 (emphasis added).

Since the ten horns are on the seven heads, we can safely conclude the ten kings come out of the seven heads. The seven heads are: Egypt, Assyria, Babylon, Medo-Persia, Greece, Rome and Revived Rome.

The ten horns are explained in Revelation 17:

> *[12] "The ten horns which you saw are ten kings who have received no kingdom as yet, **but they receive authority for one hour as kings with the beast.**
> [13]These are of one mind, and they will give their power and authority to the beast."*
> Revelation 17:12-13 (emphasis added)

The ten kings are leaders of the revived Roman Empire. They only rule the world during antichrist's reign, the second half of the Tribulation.

Four of the above nations also ruled and/or dominated Jerusalem. The book of Daniel defines their role in very great detail in several images. We see them described as the four metals in Nebuchadnezzar's image in Daniel 2, and the four great beasts of Daniel 7. Look at the chart on the next page and compare the image in Daniel 2 with the great beasts of Daniel 7 and the countries each represents.

COUNTRY	NEBUCHADNEZZAR'S IMAGE (DANIEL 2)	FOUR GREAT BEASTS (DANIEL 7)
Babylon (Iraq)	Head-gold	Lion
Medo-Persia (Iran)	Chest and Arms-silver	Bear
Greece	Belly and Thighs-bronze	Leopard
Rome	Legs-Iron Feet and Toes-iron and clay	Dreadful Beast

These four nations are also represented by the four chariots of Zechariah and the four horsemen of Revelation 6. They will reap great judgment for their treatment of God's chosen people, the Jews. But before they are judged, they will again deal severe body blows to believers and Jews who are on the earth during the Tribulation. To get an overview of things to come, let us look more closely at the feet of iron and clay, and then the dreadful beast.

The ten toes of iron and clay represent the ten final kings:

> *⁴¹Whereas you saw the feet and toes, partly of potter's clay and partly of iron, **the kingdom shall be divided**; yet the strength of the iron shall be in it, just as you saw the iron mixed with ceramic clay.*
>
> *⁴²And as the toes of the feet were partly of iron and partly of clay, so the kingdom shall be partly strong and partly fragile.*
>
> *⁴³As you saw **iron mixed with ceramic clay**, they will mingle with the seed of men; but **they will not adhere to one another**, just as iron does not mix with clay.*
>
> Daniel 2:41-43 (emphasis added)

"The kingdom shall be divided" Daniel 2:41, but *"they will not adhere to one another,"* Daniel 2:43.

The iron in the feet and toes must be the revived Roman Empire. The legs of iron were the ancient Roman Empire. The iron in the feet represents democracies in the European Union.

The "feet" of iron and clay rule in the first 3 ½ years of the Tribulation. The European Union dominates the world, and it has many members. The clay is Islam. **The "toes" of iron and clay** are the ten kings. They only rule during the second 3 ½ years of the Tribulation with the beast. They receive authority for one hour (Revelation 17:12).

The clay, or Islam, is described in the King James Version as "partly broken." (Daniel 2:42). This may symbolize the lack of unity between the Shi'ite and Sunni Moslems, or it may illustrate that the antichrist has to "break" three Islamic nations, Egypt, Libya, and Ethiopia before they follow him (Daniel 11:43).

THE FEET OF IRON AND CLAY:

SUBSTANCE	REPRESENTS	DANIEL 2:42
Iron	Democratic Revived Roman Empire/ Apostate Church	Strong
Clay	Dictatorship/Islam	Broken (KJV)

The Christianity (feet of iron), which aligns itself with Islam (feet of clay), is in fact the apostate Church. Even in apostasy, they cannot successfully mix their doctrine with the beliefs of the Moslems. Thus, as we shall see in Chapter 11 of this book, the apostate Church is devoured by fire three and one half years into the Tribulation.

Now we shall consider the dreadful beast.

> [7]*After this I saw in the night visions, and behold, a fourth beast, dreadful and terrible, exceedingly strong. It had huge iron teeth; it was devouring, breaking in pieces, and trampling the residue with its feet. It was different from all the beasts that were before it, **and it had ten horns**.*
>
> Daniel 7:7 (emphasis added)

It is my view that the European Union is emerging as the dreadful beast, even as I write this book.

Daniel continues the description.

> *²³Thus he said: "The fourth beast shall be a fourth kingdom on earth, Which shall be different from all other kingdoms, And **shall devour the whole earth**, trample it and break it in pieces.*
> *²⁴The ten horns are ten kings **Who shall arise from this kingdom**. And another shall rise after them; He shall be different from the first ones, And **shall subdue three kings**."*
>
> Daniel 7:23-24 (emphasis added)

The Bible does not say that the ten kings will be a confederation of ten nations, as some have taught. **Rather, the Bible says ten kings "shall arise" from the fourth kingdom** (Daniel 7:24). This kingdom is "different" from all other kingdoms. Is it possible that "different" might mean many diverse nations governed by one constitution, the European Union? **Notice that the total number of kings in the fourth kingdom is not given in the Bible.**

Three of these kings will be "subdued" mid-Tribulation. Then "another shall arise after them," the antichrist. **He is not one of the original ten kings**. Ultimately this beast shall "devour the whole earth." Another passage in the book of Revelation confirms our worst fear. This will, indeed, be a global dictatorship.

> *⁷It was granted to him to make war with the saints and to overcome them. And authority was given him over **every tribe, tongue, and nation**.*
>
> Revelation 13:7 (emphasis added)

However, the Word also teaches that some countries escape his dominion (Daniel 11:41), and some rebel against him. (Daniel 11:44). Many who do not succumb will pay with their lives. (Revelation 20:4) It is a small price to pay for eternal life.

Next, let us direct our attention to the three kings who need to be subdued. They threw their lot in with the European Union at the beginning of the Tribulation (see page 80).

However, the antichrist will not seize power until mid-Tribulation. The length of his reign of terror is only forty-two months (Revelation 13:5).

Daniel 11 describes the events that unfold mid-Tribulation, as the antichrist seizes power and subdues three Kings:

> ⁴⁰*At the time of the end the king of the South (Egypt) shall attack him (antichrist); and the king of the North (antichrist) shall come against him (Egypt) like a whirlwind, with chariots, horsemen, and with many ships; and he shall enter the countries, overwhelm them, and pass through.*
> ⁴¹*He (antichrist) shall also enter the Glorious Land (Israel), and many countries shall be overthrown; but these shall escape from his hand: Edom, Moab, and the prominent people of Ammon (Jordan).*
> ⁴²*He shall stretch out his hand against the countries, and the land of Egypt shall not escape.*
> ⁴³*He shall have power over the treasures of gold and silver, and over all the precious things of Egypt; also the Libyans and Ethiopians shall follow at his heels.*
>
> Daniel 11:40-43
> (parenthesis author's interpretation)

Therefore, we conclude that the three kings who are coerced into following antichrist are Egypt, Ethiopia and Libya. It is our unproven theory that these staunch Islamic states, which have pledged themselves to Allah, will not appreciate the antichrist's demand that they now worship him.

Let us now sift through the information we have compiled:

1. We wish to identify ten kings.
2. The ten toes on Nebuchadnezzar's image represent them. Since each foot has five toes, each half of the Roman Empire will represent five kings. We divide the kingdom at Israel. Geographically, five kings will reign from countries east of Israel; five kings will reign from countries west of Israel.

3. There will be Islamic dictatorships and democracies of the EU in both the west and the east. **This must be true because both feet are partly iron and partly clay** (Daniel 2:41-43).
4. Six of the kings are identified as: Egypt, Assyria, Babylon, Medo-Persia, Greece, and Rome (see page 101).
5. Three kings must be subdued. They are: Egypt, Libya, and Ethiopia. (Biblical Ethiopia may be modern Sudan. Notice Egypt is mentioned in both lists).

Based on the above, I conclude that the Bible gives us eight of the ten kings who will rule at the end of the age. They are:

Western Kings	Eastern Kings
Rome (Italy)	Egypt
Greece	Assyria (Syria & Turkey)
Libya	Babylon (Iraq)
	Medo-Persia (Iran)
	Ethiopia

In the interest of intellectual honesty, we must admit that most of Iran was not considered a part of the Roman Empire, although the borders were fluid. The ancient Persian Empire was rather considered an ally of Rome. However, because it is one of the seven ancient empires (one of seven heads) out of which the ten horns come, I have included it.

The ancient Assyrian Empire included portions of Turkey, Syria, Iraq, and Iran. Since we have listed Iraq and Iran as two of the kings, we will focus here on Turkey and Syria. It is my view that Turkey will be one of the ten kings. Let us now consider the antichrist, also from Assyria:

> [7]*...And another shall rise after them; he shall be different from the first ones,...*
>
> Daniel 7:24

This king, the antichrist, will arise from the Assyrian Empire. (Micah 5:5-6) He will be from Syria, and he will ultimately rule the ten kings (see page 39).

On the western side of the empire, two of the kings are not listed in the Bible, as far as I can ascertain. Most scholars believe that the revived Roman Empire will approximate the borders of the ancient Roman Empire.

To put the emerging Roman Empire (also called the European Union) into perspective let us consider the words of Dr. Billye Brim: "The European Union is Franco-German driven. They are the big voices in the EU, so what France and Germany exhibit is what's going to occur on a widespread basis."[16]

At first glance, it is tempting to list France and Germany as the other two western kings. There is a difficulty with Germany. They were neither a part of the ancient Roman Empire nor an ally. Rome tried to dominate the Germans and failed. Therefore, I choose to omit Germany as a western king. Two possible reasons the now powerful Germany may not be one of the ten kings are the following:

> "...Germany may not be one of the ten kings..."

1. Having lost eighty-four percent of their soldiers in the Ezekiel War, they have been severely weakened (see page 74).
2. God has chosen to spare the homeland of Martin Luther, the founder of the Protestant movement.

Therefore I consider the following countries candidates for the other two western kings: France, England, Spain, or Belgium. If required to choose, I would pick Spain and France.

In the middle ages, the spread of Islam through northern Africa and into Europe was halted in Spain. Since then, the Moslems have desired to regain the initiative and control the entire Iberian

Peninsula. In 2004 Moslem terrorists bombed railroad cars in Madrid right before the nation's elections. The resulting fear that fell over the Spanish people tilted the election results. They threw out the pro-democracy government and brought in the socialists. The new Spanish government immediately withdrew its troops from Iraq, alienating itself from the American led coalition. Thus the Spanish government, once a staunch U.S. ally, is now possibly a candidate to be the "9th King" of the revived Roman Empire.

It is my opinion that France is a likely candidate to rule as the 10th king. As Billye Brim has said, France is the big voice in the European Union. As a postmodern, post Christian, and anti-semitic state, it is a poster child for all that is wrong with Europe. France has embraced secularism. Church attendance is rare. France was once home to Ayatollah Khomeini, and presently houses Yasser Arafat's wife. In the 1980's they exported a nuclear reactor to Iraq and were staunch supporters of Saddam Hussein. Execution by guillotine was practiced in France into the 19th century. Beheading will be revived as a method of execution during the Tribulation (Revelation 20:4). Furthermore, France considers the Arabs the rightful owner of Israel (Palestine to them), and always votes with the Arabs and against the Jews in the United Nations.

As history continues to unfold, I may be proven wrong. The reader is invited to consider alternative ideas. The primary purpose for speculating about the final ten kings is this: **We wish to enlist you, dear reader, in prayer for these unholy nations.** We will meet them again in Chapter 11, where their diabolical role during the Tribulation will be further exposed.

Candidates for the ten kings of the revived Roman Empire are listed in the chart on the next page.

GEOGRAPHIC LOCATION	MODERN NATION	ANCIENT ROMAN NAME	ANCIENT BIBLICAL NAME
WEST	Italy	Rome	Rome
	Greece	Grecia	Greece
	Libya	Tripolitania	Libya
	Spain*	Hispania	None given
	France*	Gallia	None given
EAST	Egypt	Egypt	Egypt
	Turkey & Syria	Asia	Assyria
	Iraq	Mesopotamia	Babylon
	Iran	Armenia, Parthia	Medo-Persia
	Ethiopia	Nubia	Ethiopia

*Author's Opinion

Revived Roman Empire by continent:

Europe: Italy, Greece, Spain, France
Asia: Assyria, Iraq, Iran
Africa: Libya, Ethiopia, Egypt

What about America, the strong and righteous nation that has defended the poor and weak for so long? It is our unproven theory (and fervent prayer) that many of America's leadership will be raptured. Thus, America will be temporarily weakened. As she struggles to get back on her feet again, she will have to fight against activists for the following causes: gay rights, abortion, animal rights, legalization of drugs, euthanasia and radical environmental policies. No doubt God will reinvigorate her, for the sake of those who come to faith after the rapture, before the seven-year ordeal is concluded. Those of us in heaven will be cheering America onward, as she rights the ship of state and thwarts the antichrist! America and all the other nations who hope to be judged "sheep" nations (Matthew 25:33) will have many hardships to endure. Read on to see what the word of God has to say about the upcoming seven year Tribulation period, also called Daniel's seventieth week (Daniel 9:27).

CHAPTER 10
FTH

The Tribulation:
An Overview

It is the purpose of this chapter to provide a general explanation of the upcoming Tribulation. To understand each seal, trumpet, vial, plague and earthquake, the reader is encouraged to consult and study the Word of God. It is the view of many scholars that the book of Revelation is, for the most part, in chronological order. **God is the Perfect Father; He is not trying to confuse His people!**

The next two pages contain a chart that will assist the reader in understanding the Tribulation.

EVENT	WRATH OF THE LAMB
WILL BEGIN*	Probably in September - October
DURATION	3 ½ years Revelation 11:3
DISCUSSED IN	Revelation Chapters 6–9 and 11:15
AREA AFFECTED	1/3 of the Earth [Area of 10 Kings plus Russia] Revelation Chapters 8:7–12 and 9:18
FIRST EVENT	The 4 horsemen released Revelation Chapter 6:1-8
THIRD HEAVEN SEEN ON EARTH	An open heaven God's Throne seen Revelation 6:14-16
EVENTS INCLUDE	7 Seals, 7 Trumpets Revelation Chapters 6-10
JUDGMENTS ORDERED BY	Jesus Revelation 6:16
ROLE OF EUPHRATES RIVER	4 Angels released with 200,000,000 man army, probably an Islamic army* Revelation 9:13-16
PRIMARY PREACHERS IN THE ERA	Enoch, Elijah, and 144,000 Jewish witnesses Revelation 7:5-8 and 11:3
CULMINATES IN	3 Woes and End of 6th Millennium - Revelation 11:15, 18 1st Woe Revelation 9:2, 11-12 2nd Woe Revelation 9:14 and 11:7, 14 3rd Woe Revelation 12:12

* denotes author's opinion

EVENT	WRATH OF JEHOVAH
WILL BEGIN*	Probably in March - April
DURATION	3 ½ years Revelation 13:15
DISCUSSED IN	Revelation Chapters 14–16 and 18
AREA AFFECTED	Entire World Revelation 13:3; 13:7; Zechariah 12:3; Daniel 7:23; Jeremiah 25:26; Joel 3:2
FIRST EVENT	Antichrist seizes Jerusalem Revelation 11:7; Daniel 11:41a, 45
THIRD HEAVEN SEEN ON EARTH	An open heaven God's Tabernacle and Ark seen Revelation 11:19; 13:6; 15:5
EVENTS INCLUDE	7 Vials (also called bowls) Revelation Chapters 15 & 16
JUDGMENTS ORDERED BY	God the Father Revelation 15:1 and 16:1
ROLE OF EUPHRATES RIVER	River dries up Kings of the east march forth 6th vial, Revelation 16:12
PRIMARY PREACHERS IN THE ERA	Angels and Jesus Himself Revelation 14:6–13; 16:15
CULMINATES IN	Jesus returns with the saints on Mt. Olive Revelation 19:11–14; Isaiah 52:7; Nahum 1:15; Zechariah 14:4; Jude 14, 15
* denotes author's opinion	

The first three and a half years of the Tribulation are called the "Wrath of the Lamb." The judgments (except the spread of Islam - see page 72) are confined to Israel's enemies. Notice that those judgments come to a third part of the earth:

> [7]*...the third part of the trees was burned up...*
> [8]*...the third part of the sea became blood...*
> [9]*...the third part of the creatures which were in the sea, and had life die...*
> [10]*...a great star from heaven...fell upon the third part of the rivers...*
>
> Revelation 8:7-10 KJV

> [12]*...the day shone not for a third part of it (the earth)...*
>
> Revelation 8:12 KJV
(parenthesis author's opinion)

> [18]*By these was the third part of men killed, ...*
>
> Revelation 9:18 KJV

Many scholars agree that these are not judgments on a literal third of human beings and nature. Since this is the Wrath of the Lamb (Jesus), we see this as a destruction on *some* trees, *some* animals and *some* human beings who occupy one third of planet earth. Remember that Jesus judges those who mistreat the Jews.

> [40]*"...inasmuch as you did it to one of the least of these My brethren, you did it to Me."*
>
> Matthew 25:40

See Micah 5:3 for a better understanding of the word "brethren."

The European Union only represents one fourth of the world. But the Wrath of the Lamb will judge "a third part" of the world. Thus we include Russia in these judgments, just as we included Russia in the famine that followed the Ezekiel War (see page 74).

Although Russia is not an ancient enemy of Israel, historically their record against Israel has been abysmal. Under the Czars in the 1800's there were many pogroms (massacres of Jews and destruction of their property) in Russia. Beginning in 1881, the

May Laws herded Jews into Russian ghettos. After the Communists took control in 1917, the Jews were trapped in this hostile land. When the Jewish state was founded in 1948, Russian Jews desired to go home. The Communists forbade it.

Of course, God had foreseen all of this, as Isaiah had prophesied 2 ½ millennia earlier. The Jews would return to Israel freely from the East and West; but He would have to order the North (Russia) to give them up. God fulfilled this prophecy when He sovereignly dismantled Soviet Communism in 1989.

> *⁵Fear not, for I am with you; I will bring your descendants from the east, And gather you from the west;*
> **⁶I will say to the north, "Give them up!'…"**
>
> Isaiah 43:5, 6 (emphasis added)

Therefore, we include Russia in the third of the earth that will be judged during the Wrath of the Lamb. This era will conclude with the last three trumpets, which are also called the "three woes."

I see the woes, exclamations of grief, as relating to demonic invasion into earthly affairs:

1. First woe - the release of Apollyon, a Grecian evil prince
2. Second woe - the release of the four evil demon princes of Egypt, Assyria, Iraq and Iran
3. Third woe - the casting of satan, the prince of the power of the air, to earth

THE FIRST WOE (Revelation 8:13; 9:1–12)

The king of the bottomless pit is released with his hordes to torment men for five months. Both the Hebrew name, *Abaddon*, and the Greek name, *Apollyon*, of this evil spirit are given. He is the demon who may soon indwell the antichrist. Is it possible that he is the ancient prince of Greece spoken of in Daniel 10:20? Since the antichrist will be a Syrian Greek, (see page 36) I would not be surprised to see this Grecian demon possessing him.

I expect that Apollyon, and not satan, indwells the antichrist because of the following:

1. Apollyon is called *"the angel of the bottomless pit"* (Revelation 9:11).
2. Antichrist is referred to as *"the beast from the bottomless pit"* (Revelation 11:7; 17:8).
3. Apollyon is referred to as having ascended out of the bottomless pit (Revelation 9:2,11); antichrist is referred to as having ascended out of the bottomless pit (Revelation 17:8).
4. Antichrist and satan are seen as separate entities throughout Revelation (Revelation 13:4; 16:13; 19:20; 20:2).
5. Apollyon is known in ancient Jewish writings and is sometimes referred to as *Asmodeus*, the prince of demons.

THE SECOND WOE (Revelation 9:12–19; 11:7–14)

The second woe includes the release of the four evil angels bound at the Euphrates River and the murder of the two witnesses by the antichrist, after which he seizes Jerusalem. The two witnesses had ordered plagues and drought against Israel's enemies. The evil world rejoices when they're slain, and sends each other gifts. Antichrist's stellar rise to fame is global! For the first time since Alexander the Great, one man will rule the world.

> **Antichrist and satan are seen as separate entities throughout Revelation.**

But who are the four evil angels who were released from the Euphrates? The six ancient enemies of Israel were each led by an evil angel. The Roman evil angel is the driving force behind the European Union. The Greek evil angel, Apollyon, could be the spirit that indwells the antichrist. Where are the evil angels who ruled ancient Egypt, Assyria, Babylon, and Medo-Persia? Could it be that they are still bound at the great river?

During the second woe, the order goes out:

> [14]*...Release the four angels that are bound at the great River Euphrates.*
>
> Revelation 9:14

Is it possible that these are the four ancient evil spirits that ruled Egypt, Assyria, Babylon and Medo-Persia? These angels gather an army of two hundred million horsemen by whom were killed *"the third part of mankind..."* (Revelation 9:18 KJV). Biblical evidence that this is an Islamic army is compelling.

1. Chronologically, we are approaching the middle of the Tribulation Period. The European Union still rules the world (Daniel 7:7), but the Islamic antichrist will soon take over (Daniel 7:8). The army of Revelation 9:16 is being assembled to defeat the European Union.

2. The assignment of this army is *"...to slay the third part of men"* Revelation 9:15 KJV. As we have already discussed, the European Union and Russia comprise a third part of men.

3. The horses in this army have heads *"...like the heads of lions;"* (Revelation 9:17). The lion is the ancient symbol of Babylon, the headquarters of the antichrist (Isaiah 14:4).

4. The army of Revelation 9:16 defeats *"...the third part of men..."* (Revelation 9:18) as we have already stated. They are identified as the European Union and Russia. The sins of the third part of men sounds like the sins of the decadent western culture. Notice that the lifestyle and sins of those who are attacked by this army includes the following (Revelation 9:20, 21):

worship demons	*satanism*
worship idols of gold and silver	*materialism*
worship idols of stone and wood	*pantheism*
sorcery	*drugs and occultic practices*
murder	*abortion, euthanasia*
sexual immorality	*sexual perversion*

This lifestyle is reminiscent of the ancient Roman Empire and sadly, the modern European Union.

Therefore we conclude the army of Revelation 9:16 is probably an Islamic army led by the Assyrian antichrist. As they conquer

Europe, recall that Moslems do not smoke, drink, take drugs, worship idols, allow nudity or other excesses of western culture. In their thinking, Allah is granting them world dominion because of their "purity."

For those Bible scholars who are looking for a Chinese army, I submit to you that the Chinese (and/or Japanese) are not involved until the second half of the Tribulation, as recorded in both Daniel and Revelation.

> *⁴⁴But news from the east and the north shall trouble him; therefore he shall go out with great fury to destroy and annihilate many.*
>
> Daniel 11:44

> *¹²Then the sixth angel poured out his bowl on the great river Euphrates, and its water was dried up, so that the way of the kings from the east might be prepared.*
>
> Revelation 16:12

The two witnesses who are killed (Revelation 11:7) are believed by most scholars to be Enoch and Elijah, who have never died (Hebrews 9:27). For three and one half years they had discipled and led 144,000 Messianic Jewish evangelists. After the rapture, the Jews took over the task of winning the world to Jesus, in union with the underground Church (Revelation 11:7–12). The 144,000 witnesses must also be raptured, since they are seen in heaven in Revelation 14:1 when the Wrath of Jehovah begins.

And so in the middle of the Tribulation, as referenced in the prologue, the Mystery of God will be finished. We believe the words *"there should be time no longer"* refers to the end of the sixth millennium:

> *⁶And sware by him that liveth for ever and ever, who created heaven, and the things that therein are, and the earth, and the things that therein are, and the sea, and the things which are therein, **that there should be time no longer:***
> *⁷But in the days of the voice of the seventh angel,*

> *when he shall begin to sound, **the mystery of God
> should be finished**, as he hath declared to his
> servants the prophets.*
>> Revelation 10:6-7 KJV (emphasis added)

The Mystery of God includes the assignment of the Church to preach to the principalities and powers in the heavens:

> *⁹and to make all see what is the fellowship of the
> mystery, which from the beginning of the ages has
> been hidden in God who created all things through
> Jesus Christ;*
> *¹⁰to the intent that now **the manifold wisdom of God
> might be made known by the church to the
> principalities and powers in the heavenly places.***
>> Ephesians 3:9-10 (emphasis added)

The seventh trumpet, also called the third woe, will topple satan and his minions from the heavenlies. Thus, that preaching assignment of the Church has concluded:

> *⁷And war broke out in heaven: Michael and his
> angels fought with the dragon; and the dragon
> and his angels fought,*
> *⁸but they did not prevail, not was a place found for
> them in heaven any longer.*
> *⁹So the great dragon was cast out, that serpent of
> old, called the Devil and Satan, who deceives the
> whole world; **he was cast to the earth, and his
> angels were cast out with him.***
>
> *¹²Therefore rejoice, O heavens, and you who dwell
> in them! **Woe** to the inhabitants of the earth and
> the sea! **For the devil has come down to you,**
> having great wrath, because he knows he has a
> short time.*
>> Revelation 12:7-9, 12 (emphasis added)

And so, like falling dominoes, the mid-Tribulation events include:

Mid Tribulation Events

1. The end of the Wrath of the Lamb and the sixth millennium.
2. The rapture of Enoch, Elijah and the 144,000 witnesses.
3. The casting of satan and his forces to earth.
4. The judgment of the saints in heaven (Revelation 11:18).
5. The flight of the Jews from Israel to Petra for three and a half years (Revelation 12:6 & 14).
6. The initiation of the Wrath of Jehovah, which begins with an open heaven:

> [17]*Saying, "We give thee thanks, O Lord God Almighty, which art, and wast, and art to come; because* **thou hast taken to thee thy great power, and hast reigned.**
> [18]*And the nations were angry,* **and thy wrath is come,** *and the time of the dead, that they should be judged, and that thou shouldest give reward unto thy servants the prophets, and to the saints, and them that fear thy name, small and great;* **and shouldest destroy them which destroy the earth."**
> [19]**And the temple of God was opened in heaven,** *and there was seen in his temple the ark of his testament...*
> Revelation 11:17-19 KJV (emphasis added)

[Note: *"Thou has taken to thee thy power and hast reigned..."* "Hast reigned" in the Greek is in the ingressive first aorist active indicative tense, which implies a momentary, completed act. It would be more accurately translated *"Thou hast taken to thee thy great power* and **begun to reign."** In other words, man's lease on planet earth has expired, and God has taken over.]

It is my view that the words *"...there should be time no longer"* (Revelation 10:6 KJV) mean that the 6,000 years of man's dominion over planet earth are finished (see page 20). Notice this prophecy is fulfilled in Chapter 11.

> [15]*Then the seventh angel sounded: And there were loud voices in heaven, saying,* **"The kingdoms of this world have become the kingdoms of our Lord**

*and of His Christ, and He shall reign forever and
ever!"*

Revelation 11:15 (emphasis added)

Who is the Mighty Angel of Revelation 10 who prophesies the
end of the sixth millennium, and the beginning of the seventh day,
the Day of the Lord? Many authors identify the Mighty Angel as
Jesus Himself. I concur for the reasons found in the chart below:

MIGHTY ANGEL OF REVELATION	SCRIPTURAL REFERENCES
1. He is clothed with a cloud. (Revelation 10:1)	*"son of man, coming with the clouds..."* Daniel 7:13 *"...a cloud received Him..."* Acts 1:9
2. A rainbow was on his head. (Revelation 10:1)	In the Bible, the rainbow is always associated with Deity. Revelation 4:2,3;
3. His face was like the sun (Revelation 10:1)	*"His face shone like the sun..."* Matthew 17:2b
4. He had a little book (Revelation 10:2)	In Revelation 5:7 Jesus held a "book" (Strong's 975). Now He holds a "small book" (Strong's 974). The book is smaller (maybe because half of the judgments are completed).
5. The angel says, *"And I will give power to my two witnesses..."* (Revelation 11:3)	The angel refers to Enoch and Elijah as my two witnesses. Enoch and Elijah teach that Jesus is Messiah; therefore, they are His two witnesses. Revelation 11:3-12

And so, as I have just stated, Jesus (the Mighty Angel)
prophecies the end of the sixth millennium in Revelation 10:6. This
prophecy is then fulfilled in Revelation 11:15. God never does
anything unless He prophecies it first (Amos 3:7).

Rev 11:17

FINALLY, AFTER **6,000** YEARS OF HUMAN HISTORY, MANKIND'S RULE ON PLANET EARTH IS CONCLUDED. THE DAY OF THE LORD, FORETOLD BY EVERY OLD TESTAMENT PROPHET, BEGINS WITH THREE AND A HALF YEARS OF JEHOVAH'S WRATH. CONCURRENTLY, THE SAINTS IN HEAVEN RECEIVE THEIR REWARD. (Judgement Seat of Christ)

THE THIRD WOE

The third woe is the casting of satan and his minions from the second heaven to the earth. It is the momentous event that winds up the sixth millennium and signals the beginning of the Day of the Lord.

> *⁹So the great dragon was cast out, that serpent of old, called the Devil and Satan, who deceives the whole world;* **he was cast to the earth, and his angels were cast out with him**.
>
> *¹⁰Then I heard a loud voice saying in heaven, "Now salvation and strength, and the kingdom of our God, and the power of His Christ have come,* **for the accuser of our brethren, who accused them before our God day and night, has been cast down**.
>
> *¹²"Therefore rejoice, O heavens, and you who dwell in them! Woe to the inhabitants of the earth and the sea!* **For the devil has come down to you,** *having great wrath, because he knows that he has a short time."*

Revelation 12:9-10, 12 (emphasis added)

Let us review again the cataclysmic events at the end of this age, and the beginning of the Day of the Lord.

See chart on next page.

MID-TRIBULATION EVENT	SUPPORTING SCRIPTURE
1. End of Church Age	*"...in the days of the ...seventh angel...the mystery of God would be finished..."* **Revelation 10:6**
2. The beginning of the Day of the Lord	*"The kingdoms of this world have become the kingdoms of our Lord and of His Christ..."* **Revelation 11:15** *"O Lord God Almighty...You have taken your great power and reigned..."* **Revelation 11:17**
3. The Wrath of God begins	*"The nations were angry and your wrath has come..."* **Revelation 11:18**
4. The saints are judged in heaven	*"...that they should be judged, and that you should reward your servants, the prophets and the saints..."* **Revelation 11:18**
5 Rapture of Enoch and Elijah	*"...'Come up here,' and they ascended to heaven in a cloud..."* **Revelation 11:12**
6 144,000 witnesses are raptured	*"...a Lamb standing on Mount Zion, and with Him 144,000..."* **Revelation 14:1**
7. An open heaven over the earth	*"Then the temple of God was opened in heaven..."* **Revelation 11:19**

Does the Church Age end with the rapture, or with the burning of Rome midway through the Tribulation? It is a question of semantics. The "glorious Church" concludes at the rapture. The "apostate Church" endures 3 1/2 more years, until it is burned by the ten kings (see Chapter 11).

Notice that the open heaven, which initiates the second half of the Tribulation, is spoken of in Revelation 11:19 and then again in Revelation 15:5. It is my view that Revelation picks up the story in 15:5 where it left off at 11:19. In other words, the mid-Tribulation events of Chapters 12, 13 and 14 run concurrently (some of it taking place in the heavenlies) with Chapter 11.

When John resumes the narrative in 15:5 he explains the seven last plagues *"...for in them the Wrath of God is complete"*

(Revelation 15:1). Thus we see the judgment is completed with an earthquake *"...and the cities of the nations fell"* (Revelation 16:19). Revelation 16:19 introduces Revelation 18, the judgment of Babylon. Jeremiah had already prophesied that the last king to be judged would be antichrist, the king of Sheshach (Babylon), in Jeremiah 25:26.

It is my belief that the book of Revelation is, in essence, in chronological order. The exception is Chapter 17, a mid-Tribulation event. Why did John insert it near the end of the book?

CHAPTER

11

FTH

A Tale of Two Burned Cities

As I just explained, for the most part, the events of Revelation are given in chronological order. The exception to this rule is Chapter 17, which deals with the burning of Rome. Rome is actually burned mid-Tribulation, in conjunction with the events of Revelation Chapter 11, 12 and 13. There are several possible reasons for inserting this mid-Tribulation catastrophe near the end of the Book of Revelation.

1. The apostate Church, headquartered in Rome, is the harlot that sits on the seven-headed beast, the antichrist (Revelation 17:3). The antichrist is not introduced until Revelation 13. Therefore, **the woman sitting on the beast could not be identified until we know who the beast is**.

2. The author wishes to compare the burning of Rome (Revelation 17) with the burning of Babylon (Revelation 18). Putting them in successive chapters helps to draw the analogy.

3. God is making a statement about His Holy City. The Babylonians burned Jerusalem in 586 B.C. The Romans burned Jerusalem in 70 A.D. Let this be a warning to every kingdom that comes against God's City: You will reap what you have sown!

The Bible interprets itself. When the Bible says *"...Babylon the great is fallen..."* (Revelation 18:2) there is no reason to believe that the Word is referring to any place on earth **except Babylon**.

According to the prophet Zechariah, prosperity will return to Shinar (Babylon) in the end times (Zechariah 5:5-11). The modern name for Babylon, is of course, Iraq.

Only in the last few years have we seen current events line up with this ancient prophecy. President Bush and the American military are attempting to bring forth a fledgling democracy in Iraq as we write this book. I expect this effort to be successful, at least for a while. As in all countries, democracy produces prosperity. The Bible clearly speaks of prosperity in Babylon (Iraq) during these end times. This wealth includes the buying and selling of:

> *[12] merchandise of gold and silver, precious stones and pearls, fine linen and purple, silk and scarlet, every kind of citron wood, every kind of object of most precious wood, bronze, iron, and marble;*
> *[13] and cinnamon and incense, fragrant oil and frankincense, wine and oil, fine flour and wheat, cattle and sheep, horses and chariots, and bodies and souls of men.*
>
> Revelation 18:12-13

> *[23] ...For your merchants were the great men of the earth, for by your sorcery all the nations were deceived.*
>
> Revelation 18:23

According to <u>Strong's Concordance</u>, sorcery includes "drugs, incantations, charms, and magic." The occult practices of Babylon as well as Iraq's perennial hatred of the Jews will cause the Lord to pronounce a most severe judgment against her. In fact, after the Tribulation, no human being will ever inhabit Babylon again.

> *[49] As Babylon has caused the slain of Israel to fall, So at Babylon the slain of all the earth shall fall.*

> *[62] "then you shall say, "O Lord, You have spoken against this place to cut it off, so that none shall remain in it, neither man nor beast, but it shall be desolate forever."*
>
> Jeremiah 51:49, 62

I therefore conclude, as I have just explained, that Revelation Chapter 18 is not allegorical. It is to be believed as literal punishment on literal Babylon, beginning at the end of the Tribulation and continuing on in perpetuity.

Before we discuss Revelation Chapter 17, it will be helpful for the reader to consider the chart on the next page.

Two Burned Cities

COMPARE AND CONTRAST CHAPTERS 17 & 18		
Category	Revelation 17	Revelation 18
Geographic Area	Rome (9, 18)	Babylon (2, 10)
Primary Role of City	Religious Center of the Apostate Christian Church (Matthew 13:33)	Economic Center of Antichrist's Government (Zechariah 5:5-11, Revelation 18: 15-16)
Judgment Announced	One of angels with seven bowls (1)	Another angel, having great authority (1)
Judgment	City burned (16)	City burned (18)
Judged Because*	Burned Jerusalem in 70 A.D.	Burned Jerusalem in 586 B.C.
Burned By	Ten Kings (16)	God Himself (8)
When Burned	Mid Tribulation (12, 16)	End of Tribulation (Revelation 16:17-19)
Her Sins	Idolatry (2) Martyrs the Saints (6) Apostasy (Matthew 13:33)	Idolatry (3) Martyrs the Saints (24) Sells men (13) Sorcery (23) Illicit Commerce (Zechariah 5:8)
Attitude of Ten Kings	Hate Her (16)	Lament for her (9)
Length of Judgment	Not Given	Forever (21) (Isaiah 34:9-10; Jeremiah 51:58,62)

*Denotes Author's Opinion

Let us now consider Revelation Chapter 17, the saga of "Mystery Babylon" (verse 5). Remembering that God is the Perfect Father, we know it is not His purpose to confuse us. As is His custom when He is revealing a mystery, He sends an interpreter, in this case an angel (verse 7). The woman in this

The woman, who is the apostate church, is sitting on the antichrist.

chapter is the apostate Christian Church, as we shall soon see. Jesus had referred to her in a parable (remember leaven always represents sin when used in the word of God).

> [33]*Another parable He spoke to them: "The kingdom of heaven is like leaven, which a woman took and hid in three measures of meal till it was all leavened."*
>
> Matthew 13:33

David Baron explains what leaven is and how to stop its growth: **Leaven** consists of a microscopic vegetable ferment, which is characterized chiefly by rapidity of its growth and diffusiveness, so that it permeates the whole lump into which it is put, and **nothing is able to stop its growth except fire — a fit emblem, therefore, of corruption, of which it is the figure in every place in which it is mentioned in the New Testament**[17] (emphasis added). As the action of leaven is destroyed by fire, the apostate Church will ultimately be destroyed by fire.

The woman, who is the apostate Church, is sitting on (that is, has the approval of) the antichrist, an Islamic military leader.

> [3]*...And I saw a **woman sitting on a scarlet beast** which was full of names of blasphemy, **having seven heads and ten horns.***
>
> [4]*The woman was arrayed in purple and scarlet, and adorned with gold and precious stones and pearls, having in her hand a golden cup full of abominations and the filthiness of her fornication.*
>
> Revelation 17:3-4 (emphasis added)

She exists during the first half of the Tribulation. At this time, the antichrist is only dominant in the Islamic world (see page 70). The Roman (seventh) Kingdom is still reigning on the earth. (Revelation 17:10) Paganism, goddess worship, and pantheism will unite with a false (apostate) Christianity in the Roman Empire. Christianity in the European Union will include a return to ancient pagan mystery religions. John describes the woman of Revelation:

> *⁵And on her forehead a name was written:*
> *MYSTERY BABYLON THE GREAT, THE MOTHER*
> *OF HARLOTS AND OF THE ABOMINATIONS*
> *OF THE EARTH.*
>
> Revelation 17:5

Harlotry in the Bible always implies worship of a false god. Has the Church compromised with Islam and paganism? We know that Moslems will behead those who resist their doctrine (Revelation 6:4; 20:4). We see the apostate Church, the woman, is also martyring the saints.

> *⁶I saw the woman, drunk with the blood of the saints*
> *and with the blood of the martyrs of Jesus. And*
> *when I saw her, I marveled with great amazement.*
>
> Revelation 17:6

What a devastating, gut-wrenching scenario! The Church that Jesus loved, nourished and died for, has totally sold out to the evil one. It would be impossible to believe, if it had not been prophesied by so many credible witnesses (2 Thessalonians 2:3; 2 Timothy 3:1-5; Matthew 13:33).

Because Revelation 17 is a mystery and God does not want us to be confused, he sends an angel to explain to John what he is saying. The angel says *"...I will tell you the mystery of the woman..."* (Revelation 17:7). The chart on the next page shows what John saw and how the angel interpreted it.

REVELATION	
What John Saw	**The Angel's Interpretation**
She is "...the great harlot that sits on many waters..." (17:1)	"The waters which you saw, where the harlot sits, are peoples, multitudes, nations and tongues." (17:15)
[We see here a picture of a universal church engulfed in harlotry, a false Christianity.]	
What John Saw	**The Angel's Interpretation**
She was "...sitting on a scarlet beast...having seven heads..." (17:3)	"The seven heads are seven mountains on which the woman sits" (17:9)
[The seven mountains are seen by various authors to be the seven hills of Rome or seven continents]	
What John Saw	**The Angel's Interpretation**
"...I saw a woman sitting on a scarlet beast...having seven heads and ten horns," (17:3)	"There are also seven kings." (17:10)
[Egypt, Assyria, Babylon, Medo-Persia, Greece, Rome and Revived Rome]	
"And the woman whom you saw is..." (17:18)	"...that great city which reigns over the kings of the earth." (17:18)
[This is Rome the center of the Revived Roman empire.]	

One might pose the question: Why not just address Mystery Babylon by her actual name, which is Rome? There are several possible explanations:

1. John is following a precedent set by Peter, who referred to Rome as Babylon in 1 Peter 5:13.

2. Mystery Babylon is a harlot. Harlotry in the Bible implies worship of false gods. Paganism began in Babylon, the cradle of civilization. "Mystery Babylon"

131

denotes total capitulation of the once holy Church to the powers of darkness.

3. The Apostle John called the city, "Mystery Babylon" as a code word, instead of Rome. John encodes the name to avert possible retaliation from the Roman government (see page 57).

We notice in verse 12 that one of the first official acts of the ten kings, who begin their world domination mid-Tribulation, under the authority of the antichrist, is to burn Rome. It is highly probable the antichrist requires them to destroy Rome as an act of allegiance to him.

> *12The ten horns which you saw are ten kings who have received no kingdom as yet, but they receive authority for one hour as kings with the beast.*
>
> *16And the ten horns which you saw on the beast, these will hate the harlot, make her desolate and naked, eat her flesh and burn her with fire.*
>
> Revelation 17:12, 16

Such irony! This apostate Church, which embraced the theology of the world, is ultimately destroyed by those with whom she compromised!

The apostate Church embraces the "doctrine of demons!"

Some of the compromises the apostate Church embraces, the "doctrines of demons" as it were, include the following:

1. There are many roads to God. Worship any god you want, any way you want. Goddess worship has been suppressed by a male-dominated society.

2. The Bible is a good book if it helps you. It is not the inspired word of God and is not infallible.

3. Abortion is an individual decision between a woman, her doctor, and her god.

4. Sexual perversion is an inborn trait. God made people that way and approves of their lifestyle.

5. God is finished with the Jews; the Church has replaced them.

6. Jesus was a good man and a prophet. He is not God; He did not die for our sins.

Beloved, if your Church teaches any of the above doctrines, RUN, DON'T WALK, to the nearest exit and never look back. *"There is a way that seems right to a man, but its end is the way of death"* (Proverbs 14:12). Many Christians who read this book after the rapture will recognize doctrines their Church embraced in this list. Thankfully, it is not too late for you. Search the Scriptures and repent. God still has a high call for your life. For seven cataclysmic years the Jews will suffer indignation one last time. You can still serve God. You can be their friend.

CHAPTER 12

God's Chosen People

Abraham, the patriarch had two sons, Isaac, the father of the Jews, and Ishmael, the father of the Arabs. Today there are about five hundred million Arabs, descendants of Ishmael. Yet there are less than fifteen million Jews on planet earth. What accounts for the disparate number of progeny of the two sons of Abraham? This and this alone: **Satan has dedicated himself throughout human history to destroying the Jews, God's Chosen People.**

Satan's final attempt to destroy the Jews, in tandem with antichrist, will occur during the Tribulation Period. Here is a summary of how Daniel describes that seven year period also called "Daniel's seventieth week."

> *[27]Then he (the antichrist) shall confirm a covenant (peace treaty) with many (the Jews) for one week (seven years);*
> *But in the middle of the week (three and one half years into the Tribulation)*
> *He shall bring an end to sacrifice and offering (break the treaty with the Jews and demand they desist from offering blood sacrifices to Jehovah in the rebuilt Temple).*
> *And on the wing of abominations shall be one who makes desolate, (antichrist shall set up the "abomination of desolation" [Mark 13:14] in the holy of holies and force people to worship it)*
> *Even until the consummation, (end of the*

> *Tribulation) which is determined, (by Jehovah),*
> *Is poured out on the desolate (by the return of the*
> *Messiah to punish the ungodly).*
>
> Daniel 9:27
> (parenthesis are author's interpretation)

After this time period, Jesus will rule the earth from Jerusalem during the one thousand year millennium.

As David Baron explains so eloquently in his book, <u>Zechariah: A Commentary on His Dreams and Visions</u>:

```
And this dear reader, the
establishment of Messiah's throne
of righteousness on Mount Zion, that
from it, and Israel as a center,
His beneficent rule may extend over
the whole earth and bless all
peoples, is the appointed goal of
history toward which all things are
moving.18
```

During the Millennial Age, the Jews will be highly honored in the human family. These words of Zechariah help to encourage the Jews until that great day.

> [23]*Thus says the Lord of hosts: "In those days ten men from every language of the nations shall grasp the sleeve of a Jewish man, saying, 'Let us go with you, for we have heard that God is with you.'"*
>
> Zechariah 8:23

God sees three groups of people on earth: the Jews, the nations and the Church.

> [32]*Give no offense, either to the Jews or to the Greeks (nations), or to the church of God,*
>
> 1 Corinthians 10:32
> (parenthesis are author's interpretation)

Throughout human history, God, Who is the perfect Father, has used both of His covenant peoples, the Jews and the Church, to

136

draw the nations (gentiles) to Himself. The Jews and the Church have much in common regarding our relationship with the Godhead. (It is helpful to remember that the Old Testament is written primarily to the Jews and the nations. In the New Testament, God is addressing primarily the Church.)

Below is a chart, illustrating God's two covenants:

1. The Law, given to the Jews.
2. The New Covenant, grace, given to the Church.

Learn this mystery given through the great Apostle Paul.

> *[25]For I do not desire, brethren, that you should be ignorant of this mystery, lest you should be wise in your own opinion, that blindness in part has happened to Israel until the fullness of the Gentiles has come in.*
> *[26]**And so all Israel will be saved,...***
>
> Romans 11:25-26 (emphasis added)

Refer to the chart below.

WHAT THE WORD OF GOD SAYS	TO THE JEWS	TO THE CHURCH
God is their Rock	Isaiah. 44:8	1 Corinthians. 10:4
God is their First and Last	Isaiah. 44:6	Revelation. 1:8
Their power comes from the Holy Spirit	Psalm 51:11	John 20:22-23
Their purpose is to win souls	Psalm 51:12 Proverbs 11:30	Mark 16:15–16
They are a light to the world (gentiles)	Isaiah. 42:6 & 49:6	Matthew 5:14
They are married to God	Jeremiah. 3:14	2 Corinthians. 12:2 Matthew 25:1
If they repent, God will always receive them back	Jeremiah 3:12, 13	1 John 1:7-9

However, it is also true that we have different covenants, and God has separate plans for the Jews and the Church.

The world owes a great debt of gratitude for all the Jews have contributed, as the great Apostle Paul explains.

> *⁴...who are the Israelites, to whom pertain the adoption, the glory, the convenants, the giving of the law, the service of God, and the promises;*
> *⁵of whom are the fathers and from whom, according to the flesh, Christ came, who is over all, the eternally blessed God, Amen.*
>
> Romans 9:4-5

Unquestionably the greatest gift we have received from the Jews is our Lord and Savior Jesus Christ, the son of Mary, a Jewish virgin.

It is our high call to work toward perfection, using the principles given to us by Christ.

> *¹¹And He Himself gave some to be apostles, some prophets, some evangelists, and some pastors and teachers,*
> *¹²for the equipping of the saints for the work of ministry, for the edifying of the body of Christ,*
> *¹³till we all come to the unity of the faith and of the knowledge of the Son of God, **to a perfect man**, to the measure of the stature of the fullness of Christ, ...*
>
> Ephesians 4:11–13 (emphasis added)

When we have become that "perfect man" without spot or wrinkle (see pages 33 and 95), we will be caught away into heaven, before the Tribulation begins. At that time the assignment to win the lost will return to the Jews. The prophet Elijah will return to help instruct the Jews:

> *⁵Behold, I will send you Elijah the prophet Before the coming of the great and dreadful day of the Lord.*
> *⁶And he will turn The hearts of the fathers to the children, And the hearts of the children to their*

fathers, Lest I come and strike the earth with a curse.

Malachi 4:5-6

Elijah along with Enoch–the only two Old Testament prophets who have never tasted death (see Hebrews 9:27) will be given permission by God to preach for three and a half years.

> *³And I will give power to my two witnesses, and they will prophesy one thousand two hundred and sixty days, clothed in sackcloth.*
>
> *⁵And if anyone wants to harm them, fire proceeds from their mouth and devours their enemies. And if anyone wants to harm them, he must be killed in this manner.*
> *⁶These have power to shut heaven, **so that no rain falls in the days of their prophecy:** and they have power over waters to turn them to blood, and to strike the earth with all plagues, as often as they desire.*

Revelation 11:3, 5-6 (emphasis added)

They will raise up 144,000 Jewish disciples, who will help them preach the Word of God.

> *⁴And I heard the number of those who were sealed. One hundred and forty-four thousand of all the tribes of the children of Israel were sealed:*

Revelation 7:4

There will be great suffering in the Middle East, due to the three and a half year drought. Mid-Tribulation, antichrist will march into Jerusalem, murder Enoch and Elijah, and take over the Holy City.

> *⁷When they finish their testimony, the beast that ascends out of the bottomless pit will make war against them, overcome them, and kill them.*
> *⁸And their dead bodies will lie in the street of **the***

> **great city** which spiritually is called **Sodom and Egypt, where also our Lord was crucified.**
>
> Revelation 11:7-8 (emphasis added)

Notice, John immediately changes the name of the city of "Jerusalem" to "Sodom" and "Egypt," as soon as it is seized. The city has become a center of sexual immorality (Sodom) and worship of a man as god. (As Pharaoh was worshiped in Egypt, the antichrist will be worshipped in Jerusalem.)

The nations of the world will rejoice, and antichrist will begin his three and a half year reign. The nations will give their power willingly to antichrist, because he was able to kill Enoch and Elijah. As the world watches the news networks on satellite TV, they gaze in jubilation at the dead bodies of Enoch and Elijah.

> [9]Then those from the peoples, tribes, tongues, and nations will see their dead bodies three-and-a-half days, and not allow their dead bodies to be put into graves.
>
> [10]And those who dwell on the earth will rejoice over them, make merry, and send gifts to one another, because these two prophets tormented those who dwell on the earth.
>
> Revelation 11:9-10

...they gaze in jubilation at the dead bodies...

BUT GOD ALWAYS WINS!

> [11]Now after the three-and-a-half days the breath of life from God entered them, and they stood on their feet, and a great fear fell on those who saw them.
>
> [12]And they heard a loud voice from heaven saying to them, **"Come up here."** And they ascended to heaven in a cloud, and their enemies saw them.
>
> Revelation 11:11, 12 (emphasis added)

An earthquake ensues, during which many Jews give glory to God (Revelation 11:13). Finally the sixth millennium has ended, and the Day of the Lord begins.

> *[15]Then the seventh angel sounded: And there were loud voices in heaven, saying,* **"The kingdoms of this world have become the kingdoms of our Lord and of His Christ,** *and He shall reign forever and ever!"*
>
> *[16]And the twenty-four elders who sat before God on their thrones fell on their faces and worshiped God,*
>
> *[17]saying: "We give You thanks, O Lord God Almighty, The One who is and who was and who is to come, Because* **You have taken Your great power and reigned.**
>
> *[18]The nations were angry, and Your wrath has come, And the time of the dead, that they should be judged, and that You should reward Your servants the prophets and the saints, And those who fear Your name, small and great, And should destroy those who destroy the earth."*
>
> Revelation 11:15–18 (emphasis added)

The "Day of the Lord" begins with an open heaven. The day of the Lord is discussed in greater detail in Chapter 14.

Before we conclude our discussion of God's Chosen People, it is helpful to explain the different roles God has assigned to the Jews and the Church. Each group has a separate mandate, and we will work together during the Millennial Reign and into eternity. On the next page is a chart comparing the Jews and the Church and the role each plays.

COMPARISON BETWEEN THE JEWS AND THE CHURCH

JEWS	CHURCH
Physical seed of Abraham. Genesis 21:12	Spiritual seed of Abraham. Galatians 3:29
Seek righteousness by works. Romans 9:31-32	Receive righteousness by faith. Romans 10:9-10
Saved as a nation, at Christ's return. Romans 11:26, 27; Zechariah 12:10	Saved as individuals by confessing Jesus. Romans 10: 9
God used the Jews to save the Church. Romans 9:5	God will use the Church to save the Jews. Romans 10:19
Will rule and reign from Israel. Psalm 89:3, 4; 2 Samuel 7:12, 13; Isaiah 2:2–4	Will rule and reign from heavenly Jerusalem. Hebrews 12:22; Ephesians 2:6; Philippians 3:20

Brothers and sisters, the purpose of this chapter is to stir in your heart a deep love for the Jews, God's Chosen People. For two thousand years, "Christians" have been trying to kill them or convert them. But as the Church Age closes, the Holy Spirit is calling to the Church to fulfill the command He gave all people in Isaiah 40:1-2. Wise is the Christian who obeys these words:

> [1] *"Comfort, yes, comfort My People!" Says your God.*
> [2] *"**Speak comfort to Jerusalem**, and cry out to her, ..."*
>
> Isaiah 40:1-2 (emphasis added)

142

The Church has a glorious future, as we described in Chapter 8. Israel also has a wonderful future, as David Baron so articulately describes it.

> The Mission of the Church is to evangelize the world with a view to the gathering in of *individuals* *out* *of all nations* into its fold, **but it is reserved for restored and converted Israel as a nation to bring** *the nations* **to the knowledge of their glorious Messiah and King, and bring** **universal** *blessing* **to the world.**[19] (italics and emphasis added)

Those who desire to walk in God's perfect will must include supporting the Jews as God spoke it to Abraham four thousand years ago.

> *³I will bless those who bless you, and I will curse him who curses you; And in you all the families of the earth shall be blessed.*
>
> Genesis 12:3

Dear reader, if you are a Christian, the day will come when you must pass before the judgment seat of Christ. When you look into His Jewish eyes, will you be able to say, I have loved and served Your brethren, the Jews?

> *⁴⁰And the King will answer and say to them, "Assuredly, I say to you, inasmuch as you did it to one of the least of these **My brethren**, you did it to Me."*
>
> Matthew 25:40 (emphasis added)

CHAPTER

13

FTH

The Unholy Trinity

The unholy trinity, which joins together during the seven year Tribulation Period, has as its purpose to overthrow God, seize Jerusalem and rule the world. As God is love (I John 4:7-8), this evil trio is hatred incarnate. Although they work together, satan, antichrist and the false prophet are motivated by a selfish desire for the advancement of their own personal gain. Their cooperation with each other is motivated only out of love of self and hatred for humanity. Most Bible scholars have traditionally held that the "evil trinity" will include satan, antichrist and the false prophet.

SATAN (IMITATOR OF OUR HEAVENLY FATHER)

Also called the dragon, the deceiver and the accuser of the brethren, satan fell long before God created Adam (Ezekiel 28:13–17). By deceiving Eve in the Garden of Eden, he persuaded our first parents to turn over their authority and dominion of planet earth. (Thankfully, Jesus bought back our right to dominion with His death on the cross. Through faith, we take back our authority.) Satan and his hordes do not want men to receive the free gift of salvation through the Blood of Jesus. They have dedicated themselves, throughout human history, to destroying men's souls. Satan is very familiar with Biblical prophecy, and knows his end is near. He is enraged, because he will soon be bound in hell (Revelation 20:2). In an effort to take as many souls as possible with him, he will make a deal with antichrist to conquer and deceive the world. Many scholars believe satan will offer antichrist the same deal he tried to persuade Jesus to take.

145

> *⁵Then the devil, taking Him up on a high mountain, showed Him all the kingdoms of the world in a moment of time.*
>
> *⁶And the devil said to Him, "**All this authority I will give You**, and their glory; for this has been delivered to me, and I give it to whomever I wish.*
>
> *⁷Therefore, **if You will worship before me**, all will be Yours."*
>
> Luke 4:5–7 (emphasis added)

Jesus, of course, **declined** the evil offer. **Antichrist will accept it**.

> *²...The dragon gave him (antichrist) his power, his throne and great authority.*
>
> Revelation 13:2 (parenthesis are author's opinion)

During the first half of the Tribulation Period, satan will destroy souls primarily through three evil vehicles: paganism, Islam and the apostate Church.

> **He (satan) is enraged because he will soon be bound in hell.**

1. Paganism — This ancient religious system, worshiping nature (pantheism) has been practiced since antiquity. The sun, moon and planets were worshiped by primitive men. Today the "green" movement again worships nature and elevates animals to the status of human beings.

Ancient pagan mother-son worship was founded in the era of Nimrod (Genesis 11:4). A widely popular blasphemous novel trumpets worship of female deities. The following false deities, the stuff of mythology for generations, is now being reconstructed in post Christian Europe as true "deities," deserving of worship.

See Mother-Son Worship chart on following page.

Ancient Mother-Son Idol Worship

Country	Mother	Son
Babylon	Semiramis	Tammuz
Egypt	Isis	Osiris
Assyria	Ishtar	Bacchus
India	Isi	Iswara
Greece	Aphrodite	Eros
Rome	Venus	Cupid

2. Islam — It is the avowed purpose of radical fundamentalist (Shiite as well as Wahabi) Islam to conquer the world for Allah. Mohammad's command as he lay dying was, "Fight until all declare, there is no god but Allah, and Mohammad is his prophet." Militaristic Moslems believe Sharia law must rule the globe. Many moderate Moslems, probably a statistical majority, do not agree with Sharia law. In western countries, we see brave Moslem women speaking out against it.

Sharia law includes stonings, flagellations, hand amputation for stealing, no usury, limitations on women (need men's permission to be educated, vote, marry, drive) and the right for men to have up to four wives.

An especially egregious aspect of Sharia law is "honor killings." If a Moslem pledges a female relative to another Moslem in marriage, the female relative must comply, even if the proposed groom already has several wives. If she refuses the arrangement, her male family member may brutally murder her, a so-called "honor killing."[20]

Those who do not agree with militant Islam are executed by beheading. As we hear of more and more beheadings in the Middle East, our society is becoming numbed by its horror. As the executioner severs the head with his sword, he cries out, "Allah akbar." "Allah akbar" translates as "Allah is greater (or greatest)."

It's a comparison between Allah and Jehovah. After the rapture it shall appear, for a season, that Islam is indeed the defeater of Christianity.

3. The Apostate Church—After the rapture of the Bride of Christ, the Church that remains will fall into total apostasy, according to the Apostle Paul.

    ¹Now the Spirit expressly says that in latter times some will depart from the faith, giving heed to deceiving spirits and doctrines of demons,

    I Timothy 4:1

    ³Let no one deceive you by any means; for that Day (the Day of the Lord, the wrath of Jehovah) will not come unless the falling away comes first, and the man of sin is revealed, the son of perdition (mid-Tribulation).

    2 Thessalonians 2:3
    (parenthesis author's interpretation)

It is highly likely that the apostate Church will be controlled by a high ranking prelate who operates out of Rome, Italy (see Chapter 11). The Church has the tacit approval of the European Union to give the population *"...a form of godliness, but denying its power."* 2 Timothy 3:5. The European rulers will condescend to give the masses of people "religion" (the "opiate of the people" as Karl Marx called it). In Europe today most countries have a state Church, funded by the government. True Christians in Europe (including Fundamentalists, Pentecostals and Evangelicals) are branded as "cults" and outlawed in some countries already.

The era of the apostate Church will be only three and a half years. Mid-Tribulation, when antichrist seizes power from the European Union, he requires the ten kings to destroy the apostate Church (Revelation 17:16). The kings do this to prove their loyalty, the price required to be co-rulers with antichrist of the one world kingdom (Revelation17:12-13).

God will always have a people, however, who will not bow the knee to satan (Romans 11:3-4). The underground Church, as chronicled in the fictional <u>Left Behind</u> series, will bring in a mighty harvest during the Tribulation Period (Revelation 6:9–11).

Mid-Tribulation the apostate Church will be burned, Islam will be outlawed and paganism will be banned. A new religion will emerge, and everyone will be required to join. Dear reader, notice the aforementioned religions (apostate Christianity, Islam and paganism) have one thing in common. Namely, anyone seduced by them can escape judgment by coming to Jesus.

That is why the religion that replaces them is a thousand times more evil. Once a person accepts this religion, antichrist worship, his soul is forever lost.

> *⁹Then a third angel followed them, saying with a loud voice,* **"If anyone worships the beast, and his image, and receives his mark on his forehead or on his hand,**
>
> *¹⁰he himself shall also drink of the wine of the wrath of God, which is poured out full strength into the cup of His indignation. He shall be tormented with fire and brimstone in the presence of the holy angels and in the presence of the Lamb.*
>
> *¹¹And the smoke of their torment ascends forever and ever; and* **they have no rest day or night, who worship the beast and his image, and whoever receives the mark of his name."**
>
> Revelation 14:9–11 (emphasis added)

ANTICHRIST (IMITATOR OF OUR LORD JESUS)

Antichrist, an Islamic military leader who comes from Syria, has spent three and a half years solidifying his Islamic base (see page 70). Now he seizes Jerusalem (Daniel 11:41) and conquers Egypt, Libya and Ethiopia (Daniel 11:42-43). Before he can totally destroy the Jews, he is distracted by rebellion in the east and the north, possibly China and Russia (Daniel 11:44).

At some point before he seized Jerusalem, an attempt had been made on his life, possibly a bullet through his right eye. (Keep in mind that prophets could only use words in their vocabulary: eagles for airplanes, swords for guns, chariots for tanks, etc.)

*[17]Woe to the worthless shepherd, Who leaves the flock! **A sword shall be against his arm And against his right eye**; His arm shall completely wither, And his right eye shall be totally blinded.*
Zechariah 11:17 (emphasis added)

His life is saved, by evil supernatural power. Could it be that the false prophet, head of the apostate Church, saved his life? When antichrist's breath returned, could that be the moment he became indwelt by the evil demonic prince Apollyon (see Chapter 10)? Where Scripture is silent, we can only speculate.

...he became indwelt by the evil...Apollyon

*[3]And I saw one of his heads as if it had been mortally wounded, **and his deadly wound was healed.** And all the world marveled and followed the beast.*
Revelation 13:3 (emphasis added)

[4]...and they worshiped the beast saying, "Who is like the beast? Who is able to make war with him?"
Revelation 13:4

[7]It was granted to him to make war with the saints and to overcome them. And authority was given him over every tribe, tongue, and nation.
[8]All who dwell on the earth will worship him, whose names have not been written in the Book of Life of the Lamb slain from the foundation of the world.
Revelation 13:7-8

It is clear from the Scriptures that antichrist's remarkable recovery has given him great stature in the eyes of the world. His influence will be felt worldwide. He will be a man of great wealth (Daniel 8:24 & 11:36). As Hitler appropriated the wealth and property of the Jews in World War II, antichrist and his cohorts will confiscate the wealth of those who resist his control. One of antichrist's titles will be "King of Babylon" (Isaiah 14:4). Babylon is in modern Iraq. Notice that great wealth and commerce flow through Iraq throughout the Tribulation Period.

> [3] *...and the merchants of the earth have become rich*
> *through the abundance of her luxury.*
>
> Revelation 18:3

> [12]*merchandise of gold and silver, precious stones*
> *and pearls, fine linen and purple, silk and scarlet,*
> *every kind of citron wood, every kind of object of*
> *ivory, every kind of object of most precious wood,*
> *bronze, iron, and marble;*
> [13]*and cinnamon and incense, fragrant oil and*
> *frankincense, wine and oil, fine flour and wheat,*
> *cattle and sheep, horses and chariots, **and bodies***
> ***and souls of men.***
>
> Revelation 18:12-13 (emphasis added)

THE FALSE PROPHET (IMITATOR OF THE HOLY SPIRIT)

There are many types of the false prophet in history. The Jewish high priest, Menelaus, aided the evil Antiochus Epiphanes in the era of the Maccabeans.

The evil German bishop, Ludwig Muller, sold his soul for Hitler. As the official Reich bishop he encouraged the hapless German Christians to follow Adolph Hitler.

But the clearest picture of the false prophet is seen in Baalam, the Old Testament prophet who was stopped by God from cursing the Jews. (Numbers: Chapters 22 & 23). But Baalam succeeded in destroying the Jews; he taught them to commit sexual immorality.

Four characteristics of the false prophet we can ascertain from the Baalam model are:

1. He once was a true prophet of God (Numbers 24:2).
2. He despises the Jews and true believers. (Jude 11)
3. He gives the apostate Church permission to preach sexual immorality as not deviant, but ordained of God (Revelation 2:14).
4. He is motivated by greed (2 Peter 2:15).

Many scholars believe the false prophet will be the leader of the apostate Church. When he sees the Church will be burned mid-Tribulation, he ingratiates himself with antichrist in an effort to hold on to power. He is granted the power to perform lying signs and wonders (Revelation 13:13). As previously stated, he may be instrumental in raising antichrist back to life after a deadly head wound.

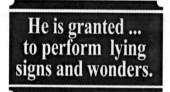

He is granted ... to perform lying signs and wonders.

The false prophet deceives the masses by the great signs he does, such as causing fire to fall from heaven to earth (Revelation 13:13). It's interesting to note that the antichrist controls him. **The false prophet is permitted to work signs only when he is in the presence of the beast** (Revelation 13:14; 19:20).

The chart on the adjoining page illustrates some aspects of the false prophet's role, which we can know for certain.

CHARACTERISTICS OF THE FALSE PROPHET	REFERENCE IN THE BOOK OF REVELATION
1. The world sees him as a "man of God," a spiritual leader.	"...he had two horns like a lamb..." (13:11)
2. His power is from satan.	"...and spoke like a dragon." (13:11)
3. He performs deceiving signs and wonders.	"And he deceives those who dwell on the earth by those signs which he was to granted to do in the sight of the beast..." (13:14)
4. His authority is limited. He can only operate in the presence of antichrist.	"...those signs which he was granted to do in the sight of the beast..." (13:14)
5. He orders men (probably scientists) to create an image to the beast.	"...telling those who dwell on the earth to make an image to the beast..." (13:14)
6. He uses his moral authority to convince the world the image is needed.	"He was granted to give breath to the image..." (13:15)
7. He orders death for those who do not worship the image.	"...and cause as many as would not worship the image of the beast to be killed. (13:15)
8. His orders extend to all of humanity, worldwide.	"He causes all, both small and great, rich and poor, free and slave..." (13:16)
9. He "seals" mankind, and all who are sealed are eternally lost. [Contrast that with God's prophet, who sealed 144,000 for Jesus at the beginning of the Tribulation.]	"...to receive a mark on their right hand or their foreheads." (13:16) [See Revelation 7:3-4]
10. He forbids unsealed people from buying food, clothing and homes, holding jobs, sending their children to school or participating in society at any level.	"...no one may buy or sell except one who has the mark or the name of the beast or the number of his name." (13:17)

The end game for the false prophet and the antichrist is the lake of fire. Many will follow them there. Dear reader, that punishment is eternal. We urge you now, if you are unsure of the final destination of your own soul, not to take any chances. Turn to page 173 of this book and bowing your knee to Jesus, ask Him to be the Lord of your life, as well as your Savior.

THE IMAGE OF THE BEAST

What or who is the image of the beast? Many theories have been forwarded. Let us begin with what the Word of God records:

1. The image is in some way representative of the antichrist. Those who worship it will be honoring the antichrist (Revelation 14:9).
2. The image, also called *"the abomination of desolation"* will reside in the Temple Holy Place (Daniel 9:27 and Matthew 24:15).
3. The image is man-made, and it's creation is ordered by the false prophet (Revelation 13:14).
4. Presumably the image is never sent to hell or the lake of fire. The Bible describes the judgment of satan (Revelation 20:2-3), the antichrist (Revelation 19:20) and the false prophet (Revelation 19:20). Since the image of the beast is not judged in the Bible, we conclude that being man-made, it ceases to be.

Why would antichrist desire an image to be created?

Many scholars believe evil supernatural forces will raise antichrist up, after he receives a deadly head wound; as we have already explained. (Zechariah 11:17, Revelation 13:3, 12, 14). He will desire to create a kingdom that will last a thousand years to simulate the one thousand year Millennial Reign of Jesus. Could this deadly wound cause antichrist to contemplate his own mortality? Could he desire an heir, but one in his image only, an image that could speak and be worshiped? (Revelation 13:15) A natural child, born of a wife, would never be acceptable. The antichrist considers women to be inferior beings (Daniel 11:37).

The false prophet comes to him with a suggestion. "Science has progressed, and we could use their technology. **You could be cloned!**"

The false prophet orders the image to be created:

> *[14]And he (the false prophet) deceives those who dwell on the earth...**telling those who dwell on the earth to make an image to the beast** who was wounded by the sword and lived.*
>
> Revelation 13:14 (emphasis added)

The word of God goes on to say:

> *[15]He was granted power to give breath to the image of the beast,*
>
> Revelation 13:15

In the New King James the word "power" is italicized because it was added at the privilege of the translator. By deleting it, we get a better understanding of this passage.

> *[15]He (the false prophet) was granted to give breath to the image of the beast,*
>
> Revelation 13:15
> (parenthesis author's interpretation)

This could be interpreted to mean this: As the "spiritual leader" of the entire world, (Revelation 13:11) the false prophet determines it is in the interest of the human family to have a successor to antichrist. Antichrist is thought to be a god. Therefore while human cloning is reprehensible to some people, consider the greater good, a guaranteed line of succession. As a spiritual guru, the false prophet has the "moral authority" to make this judgment.

In light of this possible interpretation of Revelation 13 we might also better understand a passage in 2 Thessalonians 2. This passage is addressed to those who reject the love of the truth (Jesus), during the Tribulation.

> *[11]And for this reason God will send them strong*
> *delusion, that they should believe the lie,*
>
> 2 Thessalonians 2:11

Scholars have asked the question, "What is the 'lie'?" Could the lie be this: **Antichrist is divine, and so is his image** (clone). Now the world could hardly be convinced to worship a hologram, robot, or computer that speaks. But if an infant were to speak, that would be remarkable.

As Dolly, the first cloned sheep grew to maturity at an accelerated rate, **possibly this clone of antichrist will speak while still an infant** (Revelation 13:15).

According to Moslem legend, the Mahdi (awaited one), we know as antichrist, was fully grown by the age of six and could speak from the womb.[21] (In Moslem tradition he was born in the 9th century and will reappear at the end of days.) To see antichrist's image, or cloned child, speaking as an infant, would help to confirm in the eyes of many people that they were indeed in the presence of a superior being. To those bent on getting rich by following the antichrist anyway, worshiping such a baby would be easy to do.

Let us revisit Revelation 13:15 in the King James Version.

> *[15]And he had power to give **life** unto the image of*
> *the beast, that the image of **the beast should***
> *...speak...*
>
> Revelation 13:15 (KJV emphasis added)

In Revelation 13:15 <u>Strong's Concordance</u> defines "life" as #4151, "pneuma," which means breath, or a current of air. **It is the only time in the New Testament that this word is used for life.** Most references to the word "life" in the New Testament use the Greek word "zoe," which means life. Eternal life is always referenced as eternal "zoe."

To understand "pneuma," from which we get our word pneumonia (infection in the lungs), we will use a medical analogy. A person may be clinically dead but still breathing via a respirator in an intensive care unit. A current of air is blowing in and out of the lungs and the heart continues to beat. In some cases the "zoe" life comes back and the person opens his eyes and returns to normal.

Sometimes these people say that they were "out of their bodies" for a period of time, in heaven or in hell.

What we can glean from the original Greek text is this: The image of the beast is given the ability to function as a **breathing entity**. The word for "image" is the Greek word "eikon" (Strong's Concordance #1504) which means likeness. The English word "icon" is a transliteration of eikon. We know that Jesus is the "eikon" of God (2 Corinthians 4:4).

Could it be that the beast (antichrist) in his evil desire to imitate God allows the scientific community to develop his clone, desiring an "eikon" of himself? The image of the beast will be a "breathing likeness" of the beast according to the Greek text.

In R. Edwin Sherman's book, Bible Code Bombshell, he discusses a cluster of hidden messages in Ezekiel 37. The thrust of these codes is clearly eschatological. An especially intriguing message, which could reference a cloned image of the beast reads like this: **"The newborn one is a father with no yesterday. His name will melt as bait."**[22]

This passage could reference a male child with no natural heritage. If this is the image of the beast, it is indeed bait. Those who worship it will perish, "His name will melt..." could imply that not being human, it ceases to exist after the Tribulation.

As previously mentioned, the Bible does not mention a judgment for the image of the beast. According to the Rabbi Moshe Botschko, "In my opinion, a creature born through genetic duplication is not considered human—it is clear beyond all doubt that the life form created in some scientific institution will be an animal that walks on two feet, no more."[23]

The specter of such a humanoid baby set in the Temple Holy Place is daunting. God had no part in this creation. Will men come and worship this unholy thing, bringing it gifts? It is too horrible to contemplate.

As we close this *extremely speculative* section of the text, we acknowledge that we **do not know** what or who the image of the beast will be.

Here are the facts we do know to be true:

1. The original "abomination of desolation" was placed in the Holy of Holies by Antiochus Epiphanes. It was a statue of Zeus with a face carved to look exactly like Antiochus Epiphanes.

2. Jesus is the express image of the Father.

3. Jesus affirmed an end time "abomination of desolation" would stand in the Holy Place (Mark 13:14). This could be the image of the beast.

4. Jewish folklore has always included a belief that a holy man (rabbi to them) would have the power to create a humanoid without the help of God. Such a being is called a "golem." Mary Shelley's best selling book from the nineteenth century, Frankenstein, is based on the Jewish belief that man could create life.

5. Since man was created in the image of God, he actually has extraordinary abilities. God Himself observed that man could do anything he attempted: *"...nothing that they (mankind) propose to do will be withheld from them"* (Genesis 11:6 parenthesis author's interpretation).

6. Whatever the image of the beast is, mankind will desire to worship it. God actually sends angels to be seen by men, warning them not to worship it (Revelation 14:9), **because worshiping the image of the beast causes one to be eternally lost**. The primary thrust of this section of the text is not to identify the image of the beast. It is to warn the reader, alive during the Tribulation Period, that worshiping the image of the beast will be a real temptation. In order to be found worthy to spend eternity with Jesus, you must be prepared to resist worshiping this unholy thing, whatever it is, and whatever power it displays.

666: The Number of Mankind

I began this chapter by declaring the traditional definition for the unholy trinity: satan, antichrist and the false prophet. I will now present the reader with a second view of the unholy trinity. A view that would help explain the meaning of "666."

Revelation 13 introduces three persons: the antichrist, the false prophet and the image of the beast. This chapter concludes with this enigmatic verse:

> [18]*Here is wisdom. Let him who has understanding calculate the number of the beast, for* ***it is the number of a man****: His number is 666.*
>
> Revelation 13:18 (emphasis added)

Now the words in bold type above actually say in Greek, "It is the number of mankind."[24] Therein lies the explanation of the number: 666. It is not, as some have supposed, the number of a man. It is the number of mankind, a totally human unholy trinity.

THE UNHOLY TRINITY

father	-	antichrist
son	-	image of the beast
unholy spirit	-	false prophet

Several scriptures indicate that this interpretation is accurate. The antichrist (the Bible **never** calls him the antichrist) does not try to imitate Jesus, he tries to imitate the Father.

> [3]*...the man of sin is revealed, the son of perdition,* [4]*who opposes and exalts himself above all that is called God or that is worshiped, so that* ***he sits as God in the temple of God, showing himself that he is God.***
>
> 2 Thessalonians 2:3-4 (emphasis added)

"God" in this passage is #23 in Strong's Concordance. The definition is "Theos, the supreme Divinity." In fact, every time "Theos" is used in the New Testatment it refers to the First Person of the Trinity.

And so, by declaring himself to be Theos, antichrist is declaring himself to be God Almighty, the first person of the Trinity.

The second person of the unholy trinity is the image of the beast. Remembering the Strong's Concordance #1504 shows the meaning of image as "eikon." Jesus is referred to as the "eikon" of the Father many times in the New Testament (1 Corinthians 11:7; 2 Corinthians 4:4; Colossians 1:15; Hebrews 1:3).

Could it be that the words, "eikon (image) of the beast" were put in the Scripture by the Holy Spirit to give us a clue? Jesus is the express image of the Father. Let us also consider the words of Jesus Himself when He said, *"...He who has seen Me has seen the Father;"* (John 14:9). As a cloned human being, the image of the beast is the express image of the antichrist.

King David prophesied that man would one day sever all relationships with the Godhead.

> *¹Why do the nations rage, And the people plot a vain thing?*
> *²The kings of the earth set themselves, and the rulers take counsel together, Against the Lord, and against His Anointed, saying,*
> *³***"Let us break Their bonds in pieces And cast away Their cords from us."***
>
> Psalm 2:1-3 (emphasis added)

According to Rashi, the great Jewish rabbi of the eleventh century, the fulfillment of this verse immediately precedes the coming of Messiah. Christian sources agree with that interpretation.

It's a chilling fact that a totally human trinity is already worshiped by some in the Arab world. A controversial subset of Shia Moslems, the Nusaryis, worship a group of deceased human beings. The object of their worship are Ali, Mohammad and Salman.

It could be that this trio of dead human beings worshiped as gods, foreshadow a future world religion. This new religion is represented by the number 666. This religion worships antichrist, the image of the beast and the false prophet, three human entities. This totally human trinity will only endure for three and a half years.

When Adolph Hitler realized in 1944, that he would lose World War II he ordered Germany and all occupied territories destroyed. Thankfully, most of his generals ignored his orders.

Will antichrist order the annihilation of planet earth? The Bible says if Jesus were to delay His return, all humanity would be destroyed (Matthew 24:22).

But Jesus will return, at precisely the correct moment in time. When the Father tells Him to, Jesus will leave His seat at the Father's right hand.

> [5]*The Lord is at Your right hand;*
> *He shall execute kings in the day of His wrath.*
> [6]*He shall judge among the nations, He shall fill the*
> *places with dead bodies, He shall execute the*
> *heads of many countries.*
>
> Psalm 110:5-6

Lightening will flash through the sky—lightening that begins in the east and then continues on progressing through the heavens until it reaches the west.

Men will tremble and shake with fear. Many suffer heart attacks. Women scream. The earth shakes convulsively. Nuclear bombs explode, dissolving human flesh and eyes. Hail stones the size of basketballs pelt the earth. Then a noise, an ear-splitting noise in the sky. All eyes turn toward heaven...

CHAPTER 14 FTH

Mashiach ben David

Messiah, son of David, will come out of the sky, riding a white horse, to punish the ungodly and save mankind from extinction (Matthew 24:22,30). The ancient Jewish prophet, Enoch, described His coming about 5,000 years ago. (Enoch was the great, great, great, great grandson of Adam, and the first human being to be raptured.) Jude rerecords his ancient words in the New Testament.

> *14Now Enoch , the seventh from Adam, prophesied about these men also, saying, "**Behold, the Lord comes with ten thousands of His saints,***
> *15**to execute judgment on all, to convict all who are ungodly among them** of all their ungodly deeds which they have committed in an ungodly way, and of all the harsh things which ungodly sinners have spoken against Him."*
>
> Jude 14-15 (emphasis added)

The basic belief of Orthodox Jewry was framed by Maimonides in the twelfth century A.D.

"I believe with complete faith in the coming of Messiah: and even though He tarry, I will wait for Him every coming day."

The poignancy of Messiah's coming, the premier event in all of human history, cannot be overstated. The Jews have been hated and abused throughout history. Moses himself had prophesied this would happen (Deuteronomy 28:33). When all reason for hope is gone, death and destruction are everywhere, Messiah appears out of nowhere to save the Day! The coming of Messiah in victory at the end of the age has been taught since the beginning of time (Genesis 3:15). Consider, for a moment, these faith-filled words of Job, who may have been a contemporary of Abraham.

> *25For I know that my Redeemer lives, And He shall stand at last on the earth;*
> *26And after my skin is destroyed, this I know, that in my flesh I shall see God,*
>
> Job 19:25-26 (emphasis added)

It is obvious from this passage that Job understood (probably handed down through the oral tradition) that he would one day have a glorified body. Job will receive that glorified body at the rapture. A glorified body is a flesh and bone body, like Jesus has.

> *39Behold My hands and My feet, that it is I Myself. Handle Me and see, for a spirit does not have flesh and bones as you see I have.*
>
> Luke 24:39

[Notice we will still eat and drink when we have glorified "flesh and bone" bodies. Matthew 26:29, Luke 24:43 and John 21:15]

Paul declared that ultimately, our bodies would be redeemed.

> *22For we know that the whole creation groans and labors with birth pangs together until now.*
> *23Not only that, but we also who have the first fruits of the Spirit, even we ourselves groan within ourselves, eagerly waiting for the adoption, the redemption of our body.*
>
> Romans 8:22–23 (emphasis added)

John confirms that glorious promise.

> *2Beloved, now we are children of God; and it has not yet been revealed what we shall be, but we know that when He is revealed, we shall be like Him, for we shall see Him as He is.*
>
> 1 John 3:2 (emphasis added)

The redemption of the Church and the Old Testament saints comes seven years before the redemption of the Jews. Oh, that glorious and soon-coming day! When our mortal bodies "put on" immortality, we will forever stand with Jesus as the "end time saints." We will not taste death. Dear reader, to reject this awesome testimony is to say: I would rather live in hell on earth for seven years than depart in victory and be transformed into His image.

We will not taste death!

Listen to the great apostle, Paul.

> *[22]If anyone does not love the Lord Jesus Christ, let him be accursed. O Lord, come!*
> 1 Corinthians 16:22

God showed the pagan king, Nebuchadnezzar, in a dream, the world powers that would reign during the "times of the gentiles" (see pages 55 and 103). Daniel, the greatly beloved prophet of God, was given the interpretation of this dream. Notice that the last world power to reign is the ten kings (ten toes).

The ten kings, and antichrist their leader, are not destroyed by human beings. No, dear reader, **the Church will not overcome the evil one.** The privilege of defeating the evil world system is clearly delineated in Daniel 2:45.

> *[34]You watched **while a stone was cut out without hands,** which struck the image on its feet of iron and clay, and broke them in pieces.*
> *[42]And as the toes of the feet were partly iron and partly of clay, so the kingdom shall be partly strong and partly fragile.*
> *[43]As you saw iron mixed with ceramic clay, they will mingle with the seed of men; but they will not adhere to one another, just as iron does not mix with clay.*

> *⁴⁴And in the days of these kings the God of heaven will set up a kingdom which shall never be destroyed; and the kingdom shall not be left to other people; it shall break in pieces and consume all these kingdoms, and it shall stand forever.*
> *⁴⁵Inasmuch as you saw that the stone was cut out of the mountain without hands, and that it broke in pieces the iron, the bronze, the clay, the silver, and the gold—the great God has made known to the king what will come to pass after this. The dream is certain, and its interpretation is sure.*
> Daniel 2:34, 42–45 (emphasis added)

And so we ask the question, who is the stone that destroys the evil world system? Jesus Himself is the stone.

> *¹⁷Then he looked at them and said, "What then is this that is written: 'The stone which the builders rejected has become the chief cornerstone?'*
> *¹⁸Whoever falls on that stone will be broken; but on whomever it falls, it will grind him to powder."*
> Luke 20:17-18 (emphasis added)

We recall that satan ruled the world during the seven kingdoms of this age (Egypt, Assyria, Babylon, Medo-Persia, Greece, Rome and Revived Rome). Seven is the number of completion (seven days in a week, seven notes in a scale, seven thousand years in human history). After seven kingdoms have been completed, the antichrist takes over mid-Tribulation, at the beginning of the Day of the Lord. **The antichrist kingdom is the eighth kingdom** (Revelation 17:11). Eight is the number of "new beginnings." The antichrist thinks he is setting up a one thousand year reign.

Notice the events of this three and a half year era are well chronicled, in both the Old and New Testaments. **It is Jesus, and He alone, that defeats the antichrist and the world system.**

	Old Testament	New Testament
ANTICHRIST SEIZES JERUSALEM	"...the people of the prince who is to come shall destroy the city and the sanctuary..." Daniel 9:26	"And their dead bodies will lie in the street of the great city which spiritually is called Sodom and Egypt, where also Our Lord was crucified." Revelation 11:8
ANTICHRIST DECLARES HE IS GOD	"...He shall exalt and magnify himself above every god..." Daniel 11:36	"...he sits as God in the temple of God showing himself that he is God." 2 Thessalonians 2:4
MICHAEL HELPS OUT	"At that time Michael shall stand up, the great prince who stands watch over the sons of your people..." Daniel 12:1	"And war broke out in heaven: Michael and his angels fought with the dragon..." Revelations 12:7
JEHOVAH GIVES JESUS DOMINION	"...One like the Son of Man...to Him was given dominion and glory and a kingdom..." Daniel 7:13 - 14	"...The kingdoms of this world have become the kingdoms of our Lord and of His Christ, and He shall reign forever and ever.'" Revelation 11:15
JESUS PUTS IN THE SICKLE	"Put in the sickle, for the harvest is ripe. Come, go down..." Joel 3:13	"...on the cloud sat One like the Son of Man...and in His hand a sharp sickle." Revelation 14:14
JESUS TREADS THE WINE-PRESS	"I have trodden the winepress alone..." Isaiah 63:3	"He Himself treads the winepress of the fierceness and wrath of Almighty God." Revelation 19:15b
JESUS' GARMENTS ARE BLOODY	"Their blood is sprinkled upon My garments..." Isaiah 63:3	"He was clothed with a robe dipped in blood..." Revelation 19:13
JESUS ACTS ALONE	"I looked, but there was no one to help...and My own fury, it sustained me." Isaiah 63:5	"...in righteousness He judges and makes war..." Revelation 19:11
JESUS IS LORD	"And the Lord shall be King over all the earth." Zechariah 14:9	"...and on His thigh a name written: KING OF KINGS AND LORD OF LORDS." Revelation 19:16

We recall that it was Adam, the first Jew, who fell into sin. God promised Adam and Eve that He would send His holy seed to redeem humanity (Genesis 3:15). For six thousand years, satan has been trying to destroy the Jews and abort God's plan. Satan knew that if he were successful in annihilating the Jews, Messiah would never come. Repeated agents of satan who have attempted to destroy the Jews include: Egyptians, Amalekites, Nebuchadnezzar, Haman, Antiochus Epiphanes, the Romans, the crusaders, the Spanish Inquisition, the Russian pogroms, the Third Reich, the Islamic terrorists and, very soon, the antichrist.

In some Jewish circles, Joseph, the favorite son of Jacob, is considered the "suffering Messiah." He was actually a type of the end time Messiah. Consider these facts: He was rejected by his own, sold for twenty shekels of silver, suffered unjustly and refused to sin (with Potifer's wife). When Joseph's brother finally turned to him for help (during the famine) they cried out for mercy. Joseph readily forgave them, embraced them, fed them and gave them the best land of Egypt. All these events in Joseph's life foreshadow the role of Jesus with His own brothers, the Jews. When it looks like all hope is lost, Jesus will save the day!

The climax of this book is the climax of human history. These events are all well represented in the New Testament. However, I have chosen to declare the coming of Mashiach ben David, Messiah son of David, in the words of the ancient Jewish prophets. This is my small way of honoring those who have suffered so much for so long. It is, after all, their story; it is, after all, their victory. [For dramatic emphasis, this portion of the book is in paragraph form.]

Zechariah 14:1-2; Psalms 83:4; Zechariah 14:3; Isaiah 52:7; Zechariah 14:4; Zechariah 12:10; Joel 3:16-17.

THE CLIMAX OF HUMAN HISTORY

Behold, the Day of the Lord is coming. For I will gather all the nations to battle against Jerusalem. The city shall be taken, the houses rifled and the women ravished. They (the nations) have said, "Come, and let us cut them off from being a nation, that the name of Israel may be remembered no more."

Then the Lord will go forth and fight against those nations. In that day the Lord will defend the inhabitants of Jerusalem; It shall be in that day that I (Messiah) will seek to destroy all the nations that come against Jerusalem.

How beautiful upon the mountains are the feet of Him who brings good news. And in that Day His feet will stand on the Mount of Olives, which faces Jerusalem on the east. Then they will look upon Me whom they pierced. Yes, they will mourn for Him as one mourns for His only Son, and grieve for Him as one grieves for a firstborn.

The Lord also will roar from Zion, and utter His voice from Jerusalem; the heavens and earth will shake; but the Lord will be a shelter for His people, and the strength of the children of Israel. So you shall know that I am the Lord your God, dwelling in Zion, My holy mountain.

THE DENOUEMENT

Mid-Tribulation, satan and his minions were cast to earth. Michael and his angels warred with satan. It took time. It took a war. Jesus' power is so much greater than the power of the angels. Notice how easily Jesus overpowers the antichrist.

> [8]*And then the lawless one will be revealed,* **whom the Lord will consume with the breath of His mouth and destroy with the brightness of His coming.**
>
> 2 Thessalonians 2:8 (emphasis added)

The once powerful antichrist, now totally disabled, is easily dispatched into the lake of fire, along with the false prophet.

> [20]*Then the beast was captured, and with him the false prophet who worked signs in his presence, by which he deceived those who received the mark of the beast and those who worshiped his image. These two were cast alive into the lake of fire burning with brimstone.*
>
> Revelation 19:20

The end game for unsaved people is the lake of fire.

Although some authors use the terms "hell" (bottomless pit) and "lake of fire" interchangeably, it is evident from Revelation that hell is a holding tank, so to speak, before one receives his final judgment. We recall that "death and hell" represent a place, and also two evil spirits (page 77).

The end game for the spirits "death and hell" is the lake of fire.

> [14]*Then Death and Hades were cast into the lake of fire. This is the second death.*
>
> Revelation 20:14

Likewise, the end game for unsaved people is the lake of fire. [These people's soul's are currently in hell, waiting to be reunited with their bodies, Revelation 20:13].

> [15]*And anyone not found written in the Book of Life was cast into the lake of fire.*
>
> Revelation 20:15

Satan will not be reunited with the evil duo for a thousand years. He goes to the bottomless pit (hell) to wait until the Millennium is concluded.

> [2]*He laid hold of the dragon, that serpent of old, who is the Devil and Satan, and bound him for a thousand years;*
> [3]*and he cast him into the bottomless pit, and shut him up, and set a seal on him, so that he should deceive the nations no more till the thousand years were finished.* **But after these things he must be**

released for a little while.
                    Revelation 20:2-3 (emphasis added)

There is so much more to tell. The Millennial Reign is only the beginning. The lion will lay down with the lamb and men will learn war no more. But what else?

Another war of Gog and Magog is referenced in Revelation 20:8. A time will come when the earth must be purified by fire. When will people cease to die? When will the Father Himself dwell with His people?

What Jesus prayed must be literally fulfilled.

> *[10]...Your will be done on earth as it is in heaven.*
>   Matthew 6:10

Jesus cannot be referencing the Millennial Age, since during that time there will still be some sin in the earth.

No, Jesus is speaking about eternity, which will be the first time, since the fall of Adam, that the will of God will be done perfectly on earth.

Before eternity begins, sinners must face God at the Great White Throne Judgment. They must then endure the "second death."

The primary purpose of every committed Christian, throughout the world, throughout the ages, is always the same: to take the good news of Jesus Christ to the nations. The good news is this: You do not have to go to the White Throne Judgment—you can confess Jesus to escape the judgment called the lake of fire.

Here's The Good News

The Church will be taken into heaven and Jesus wants you to be one of those who escapes (see pages 66 and 67). Being a member of the Church of Jesus Christ is not a matter of what denomination you belong to, or where you go to church. To be a member of His Church, or His Body, is determined by the intent of your heart, which only God can see. If you are unsure of your status with God, say this prayer with genuine conviction.

Heavenly Father, I know I am a sinner. Though I've fallen short of Your glory so many times, I truly believe that Jesus died on the cross so that I (<u>state your name</u>) could have eternal salvation.

Jesus, I thank you for dying on the cross for me. I invite you now to come into my heart, take over my life and show me Your will for my life. I promise that from this day forward, I will live for You and follow Your plan for my life. Fill me with Your Holy Spirit and empower me to do Your will.   Amen.

If you prayed this prayer, please write to me and I will send you a copy of the New Testament and a few suggestions on how to get started in your new life as a child of God.

Anne T. Garcia
P.O. Box 494
Columbia, IL 62236

Epilogue

When the great apostle Paul visited heaven, he saw things *"...which it is not lawful for a man to utter"* (2 Corinthians 12:4). Since Paul's day, many other people have visited heaven and then returned to their mortal bodies. By studying their work, we get a glimpse of our future life. It is the purpose of my next book to investigate what our assignment will be in the Millennium, and into eternity.

From The Hidden was always intended to be a trilogy. Part one explains the Ezekiel War and the four horsemen of the Apocalypse. Part two chronicles the tragic and exciting events of the Tribulation, culminating in the climax of God's plan. The return of Our Lord and Savior Jesus Christ, to rule and reign from Israel for a thousand years, is the centerpiece of human history.

The third and final part of this work, "It Really Is...Happily Ever After," is already being researched.

It will explore what our lives will be like in heaven. We will live in mansions; we will have jobs. We will always be happy. We need to understand these concepts and cling to them.

My youngest child used to ask me, when he was very small, "Mom, how can we go on forever? I mean...forever? How can it be?" I always answered him the same way. (I didn't tell him we are spirits, and spirits cannot cease to be. He was too young to understand that concept.) "Son," I would answer, "think of it the other way. What if we were going to have an end? How could we be happy? Knowing that we only have a million years left, then a thousand, and then finally, only one more year left to live. How could I be happy, knowing that some day I would no longer be with you?"

I guess that's why I've always loved "Amazing Grace." Has anyone ever said it better?

> "When we've been there ten thousand years,
> Bright shining as the sun.
> We've no less days to sing God's praise,
> Than when we'd first begun."

Several months ago I heard the Lord say these words: "All hands on deck." Now there are two sets of circumstances that would require the captain to call for all hands on deck: a violent storm or an enemy attack. When the Lord spoke to me, I believe He was referencing both.

I believe He was saying that He needs every Christian, in this hour, to bring in the harvest. We must be diligent to bring in the lost, in the short time we have left. So, stay the course, dear reader. *The anger of the Lord will not turn back until He has executed...the thoughts of His heart* (Jeremiah 23:20). As we walk through our role in history, and carry out our call, we will understand it perfectly.

Endnotes

[1] Jeffrey Satinover, M.D., Cracking the Bible Code, Harper Collins Publishers, Inc., New York, New York, pages 273 and 275, 1998

[2] Kenneth Copeland, Living at the End of Time— A Time of Supernatural Increase. Kenneth Copeland Publications, pages 20, 21, 22, 1997, 1998

[3] Dr. Billye Brim, "The Glory Watch", page 13, Spring 2002, A Glorious Church Fellowship, Branson, Missouri

[4] David Baron, Zechariah, A Commentary on His Visions and Prophecies, reprint, Kregel Publications, Grand Rapids, Michigan 1956, page 327

[5] Ibid, page 327

[6] Belleville News Democrat, "Divisions in Islam rooted in actions of followers after death of Mohammed," Sunday, March 23, 2003, page 7A, Belleville, Illinois

[7] Op cit Baron, page 22

[8] Ibid Baron, page 23, emphasis added

[9] Ibid pages 182, 183

[10] Ibid page 176

[11] Ibid, page 179

[12] Belleville News Democrat, "Purported Al Qaida message warns of attacks," page 5A, June 8, 2004, Belleville, Illinois

[13] Belleville News Democrat, "EU takes over policing of area," page 5A, January 2, 2003, Belleville, Illinois

[14] News Max.com Wires, www.newsmax.com/archives/articles/2003/5/27

[15] Senator Bill Frist, interviewed by Tony Snow, "Fox News Sunday with Tony Snow," Sunday, May 25, 2003

[16] Dr. Billye Brim, "The Glory Watch," page 8, Spring 2004, A Glorious Church Fellowship, Branson, Missouri

[17] David Baron, Types, Psalms and Prophecies, reprint, Keren Ahvah Meshihit, 91103 Jerusalem, Israel, page 23

[18] David Baron, Zechariah, A Commentary on His Visions and Prophecies, op cit, page 183

[19] David Baron, Israel in the Plan of God, reprint, Kregel Publications, Grand Rapids, Michigan 49501, page 283

[20] Daily Mail Newspaper, "Sisters Kidnapped," October 19, 2004, page 17, London, England

[21] "Muhammad al Mahdi," Encyclopedia of the Orient, lexicorient.com, page 1

[22] R. Edwin Sherman, Bible Code Bombshell, New Leaf Press, Green Forest, AR 72638, page 133

[23] Shahar Ilan, "Does a clone have a soul?"/ Haaretz.com, Saturday, August 6, 2005, page 1

[24] Perry Stone, Unlocking the Book of Revelation, Voice of Evangelism, Cleveland, Tennessee, 2000, page 53

Also by Anne T. Garcia

Christy's Mystery...Clues From The Hidden
You can order this story of the rapture directly from our website at
www.fromthehidden.com.

You may contact us by email at: contact@fromthehidden.com

Christy's Mystery...

Clues From The Hidden

by Anne T. Garcia

On Christmas night, everyone went to Grandma's house for dinner. Grandma used her nice dishes and new table cloth. Opened gifts were piled high, and torn wrapping paper had been stuffed in a big plastic bag and thrown away. Everybody had gotten up early this mroning to open presents

...na, you rest. We"ll do the dishes."

Call
618-281-3291
and use your
Visa or Mastercard   Only $12.99 + S/H

A colorfully illustrated children's book.
The love of a grandmother and the words
of the Bible come together to make this book the perfect gift
for any occassion!

The author combines Biblical truth with an enchanting story line
that will thrill children of all ages!

In Christy's dream, there was a
great SWOOSHING sound.
Christy was going through the
roof of the house.

Only the beginning, it really is...
Happily Ever After!

Can be purchased
online at:

www.fromthehidden.com
www.amazon.com

Back cover

CPSIA information can be obtained at www.ICGtesting.com
Printed in the USA
LVOW071945290113

317738LV00005B/279/A